My White Stepmother

by

Jayson Swann

Front Matter

To my own wonderfully unconventional family—the one that makes me laugh until my sides ache, even when they're driving me absolutely bonkers. This book wouldn't exist without the endless supply of comedic fodder you've provided, both intentional and unintentional. Seriously, you guys are a gift (even when wrapped in questionable holiday sweaters and questionable cooking choices). This one's for you. Specifically, this is dedicated to the chaotic energy of family dinners, the awkward silences that somehow become the funniest moments, and the enduring power of love that keeps us all tethered, even when we desperately want to escape to different corners of the house (or the planet).

To the countless blended families navigating the complexities of love, laughter, and occasionally questionable casserole recipes. May your path be paved with humor, understanding, and just enough wine to make it all bearable.

To the beautiful, brilliant, and occasionally bewildering women who've crossed my path and inspired this chaotic masterpiece of a story. Your strength, resilience, and impeccable sense of humor are a constant source of amazement (and comedic inspiration). You show me that love doesn't always follow a predictable script, and sometimes, the most unexpected unions result in the most rewarding outcomes. And to my own stepmother - this is not about you. This is just a book. Truly.

This book is a love letter to the messy, glorious, and sometimes utterly ridiculous world of family. May it bring you laughter, a little bit of understanding, and perhaps even a new appreciation for the wonderfully chaotic nature of human connection.

Chapter 1: A Match Made in...Chaos?

It all started with a spilled latte. Not just any latte, mind you, but a triple-shot, extra-whip, caramel-drizzled monstrosity that somehow managed to escape its flimsy cardboard prison and land, with the grace of a drunken hippopotamus, all over my crisp, new, Tommy Hilfiger shirt. 1994. Remember those shirts? Preppy perfection, until a caramel tsunami hit.

I was standing in line at "The Daily Grind," a coffee shop that smelled perpetually of burnt coffee beans and desperation, when *she* walked in. Sarah. All sunshine and bright blonde hair, a stark contrast to the gloom of the place and the general drabness of my existence. She was wearing a dress that probably cost more than my entire month's rent – a vibrant floral number that screamed "summer in the Hamptons" while I was rocking my best attempt at a "trying-to-be-cool-dad" look.

The latte incident, of course, was entirely my fault. I'd been distracted, lost in thought about my upcoming parent-teacher conference – a meeting that promised to be less about my son's academic progress and more about my questionable parenting skills. My son, little Jamal, was a whirlwind of energy, a tiny human tornado of creative destruction. The teachers were starting to refer to him as "a force of nature," which, while sounding somewhat impressive, also sounded like a euphemism for "unmanageable."

So, there I was, knee-deep in caramel-flavored despair, staring down at my ruined shirt, when a melodic laugh shattered the silence. It was Sarah. She was clutching a napkin, her eyes wide with a mixture of amusement and concern.

"Oh my god!" she exclaimed, her voice a delightful blend of Southern charm and New York sass. "I am so, so sorry! Let me help you with that."

And help me she did. Not just with the latte-stained shirt – though she did manage to scrub most of the caramel off with remarkable efficiency – but with something far more profound. She helped me see that there was more to life than overflowing laundry baskets, endless school projects, and the looming specter of another disastrous parent-teacher conference.

Our conversation that day was a whirlwind of nervous laughter and awkward silences, punctuated by the clatter of coffee cups and the low hum of the espresso machine. We talked about everything and nothing, bouncing from the merits of grunge music (she was a Pearl Jam fan, I was a die-hard Tribe Called Quest devotee) to the absurdities of dating in the 90s (think dial-up internet and agonizingly slow-paced courtship rituals).

She mentioned she was an art teacher, and I, in a rare moment of articulate self-expression, shared my struggles with being a single dad. She listened, truly listened, without judgment or the condescending pity I'd grown accustomed to. She actually seemed... interested.

There was an undeniable spark, a connection that defied logic and common sense. I, a recently widowed, Black single father navigating the treacherous waters of 90s single parenthood, and she, a white, free-spirited artist with a penchant for expensive dresses and an uncanny ability to remove caramel stains. It was, to put it mildly, unconventional.

The 90s backdrop added its own unique flavor to our burgeoning romance. Our dates were soundtracked by the smooth grooves of Boyz II Men and the angst-ridden lyrics of Nirvana. We watched "The Fresh Prince of Bel-Air" on reruns and debated the merits of different brands of sneakers (she was a Nike girl, I was a staunch Adidas supporter). These small details, these seemingly insignificant moments, weaved a tapestry of shared experience, forging a bond that transcended our obvious differences.

As our courtship progressed, the cultural differences became increasingly apparent. My apartment, a modest two-bedroom in a predominantly Black neighborhood, was a stark contrast to her stylish loft in a predominantly white area. My family, a boisterous, tightly knit group with deep Southern roots, were a far cry from her reserved, upper-middle-class family, who expressed themselves more through meticulously curated flower arrangements than heartfelt embraces.

My mother, bless her soul, was a woman who measured love in spoonfuls of collard greens and heaping helpings of fried chicken. She eyed Sarah with a mixture of suspicion and grudging curiosity. Sarah, on the other hand, was more accustomed to quinoa salads and kale smoothies. The culinary clash was inevitable, and hilarious. I still remember the time Sarah tried to make collard greens, resulting in a pot of inedible, slimy greens that resembled something you'd find growing in a swamp. The ensuing laughter, however, was more than enough to make up for the culinary catastrophe.

Introducing Sarah to my family was like dropping a brightly colored bouncy ball into a room full of meticulously placed antique furniture. There was an initial shock, a moment of stunned silence, followed by a barrage of questions and whispered comments. They were polite, of course, but the subtle apprehension was palpable. My aunt Gladys, ever the matriarch, even went so far as to ask Sarah if she knew how to cook "real food." Sarah, ever the adaptable one, simply smiled and said, "I'm a quick study."

Her family's reaction was a different breed of apprehension altogether. They were outwardly polite, but their smiles seemed strained, their conversations carefully guarded. There was an unspoken tension, a subtle hint of disapproval that hung heavy in the air. I could see the worry in Sarah's eyes, the quiet struggle to navigate the expectations of her family. It wasn't overt racism, but a quiet, ingrained discomfort with the idea of their daughter marrying a Black man. The subtle snubs, the politely veiled questions about my background, the pointed looks — they all spoke volumes.

Yet, amidst all the chaos and uncertainty, our love flourished. It was a love born not of ease but of perseverance, a love that thrived on laughter and the shared experience of navigating the complexities of our vastly different worlds. We were two people from opposite ends of the spectrum, brought together by a spilled latte and an undeniable spark. And that, my friends, is where our story truly begins.

The air in my mother's living room crackled with a tension thicker than Aunt Gladys's sweet potato pie. It wasn't the usual Sunday afternoon buzz of chatter and laughter; instead, a palpable silence hung heavy, punctuated only by the rhythmic tick-tock of the grandfather clock in the hallway. This was it. The moment of truth. The introduction of Sarah to the heart of my family, the epicenter of Southern Black tradition.

My mother, a woman whose love language was fried chicken and unsolicited advice, eyed Sarah with a mixture of suspicion and barely concealed curiosity. She'd donned her Sunday best – a vibrant purple dress that clashed spectacularly with the floral wallpaper – and her hair was sculpted into a masterpiece of tightly coiled curls. She smelled faintly of lavender and something suspiciously like hairspray – a potent combination that could clear a room in seconds. She held a plate piled high with fried chicken, her usual peace offering for any potential interloper. This time, however, the chicken seemed more like a weapon, a defensive measure against this... *pale* intruder.

Jamal, bless his cotton socks, was a whirlwind of nervous energy, flitting between Sarah and my mother like a hummingbird on a sugar rush. He'd already declared Sarah "cool," which, in Jamal-speak, translated to "not entirely terrifying," a significant achievement in his young life. My younger sister, Denise, approached the situation with the detached amusement of a seasoned observer. Armed with her ever-present notepad, she seemed more interested in documenting the social experiment unfolding before her than participating in it. She considered it anthropological research, I considered it pure nosiness.

Sarah, bless her adaptable heart, navigated this unfamiliar territory with surprising grace. She returned my mother's intense gaze with a warm smile, her blonde hair shimmering under the afternoon sun that streamed through the living room window. She accepted the offered fried chicken with a graciousness that seemed to momentarily disarm my mother. The initial tension lessened ever so slightly; at least the air was no longer thick enough to cut with a knife.

The conversation, however, was a minefield of polite small talk and veiled interrogations. My aunt Gladys, the family matriarch, a woman whose opinions held the weight of a small asteroid, launched into a detailed explanation of my mother's award-winning collard greens recipe, subtly implying that Sarah's culinary expertise likely fell far short of the mark. Sarah, ever the diplomat, listened attentively, nodding occasionally and interjecting with appreciative murmurs. I suspected she was silently calculating the odds of surviving this afternoon without culinary humiliation.

The topics ranged from the price of groceries (a clear indication of Sarah's affluence) to the virtues of different churches (a subtle inquiry into her level of religious devotion), and culminated in a spirited debate about the best method for preparing sweet potato pie. My mother insisted on a traditional recipe passed down through generations, while Sarah, surprisingly, offered a surprisingly innovative twist involving pumpkin puree and maple syrup. The discussion grew heated, a friendly battle of culinary ideologies that, for a moment, overshadowed the underlying cultural tensions.

Later that week, I took Sarah to meet her family. This was a different animal altogether. Her parents, impeccably dressed and perfectly coiffed, exuded an aura of polite distance that was both disconcerting and vaguely condescending. Their home, a picture of polished perfection, was a testament to their refined taste and considerable wealth. It was a world away from my modest apartment and my mother's bustling kitchen.

Their initial reactions were the epitome of polite, yet carefully controlled enthusiasm. They asked the standard questions: What I did for a living (phrased delicately, with a hint of underlying assessment), where I was from (the inference being that it was somehow geographically inferior), and what my family was like (the implication being that they were rather...different). Their smiles were tight, their conversations measured, and their body language spoke volumes.

Sarah's younger brother, a preppy-looking young man with an air of aloofness, barely acknowledged my presence. Her mother, while outwardly polite, carefully steered the conversation away from any mention of my background or family. It was a subtle dance of avoidance, a carefully choreographed performance designed to subtly convey their disapproval without directly confronting it.

The unspoken tension in the room was palpable. There were no boisterous arguments, no outright insults – only the chilling effect of polite disapproval, the silent judgment of a family clinging to their carefully constructed image. They weren't overtly racist, not in the blatant, shouting-from-the-rooftops kind of way. It was more insidious, a quiet, simmering prejudice woven into the fabric of their comfortable, privileged lives.

During the meal, a lavish affair that involved an elaborate presentation of several courses, the conversation remained carefully neutral. My attempts at humor were met with polite chuckles, my attempts at genuine connection with strained smiles. I felt like an anthropologist studying a rare species, an outsider observing a culture I could never fully understand.

The weekend's experiences were a stark contrast. My family's warmth, albeit chaotic and occasionally embarrassing, was genuine. Their apprehension stemmed from a protective instinct, a fear of losing me to someone they perceived as different. Sarah's family's politeness, however, felt like a carefully constructed wall, a barrier designed to keep us at arm's length.

The difference in our families' reactions was like comparing a vibrant jazz ensemble to a perfectly orchestrated string quartet. One was loud, lively, and occasionally off-key, while the other was refined, polished, and undeniably stiff. It became clear that the journey ahead wouldn't simply be about navigating a romantic relationship; it would also mean bridging two worlds that seemed irreconcilably different. The spilled latte, it seemed, had only been the beginning. The real chaos, the real challenge, was yet to come. And it all began with the very different ways two families greeted their new, quite unexpected, member.

The following week was a blur of cultural collisions. Sarah, ever the adventurous spirit, decided to embrace my family's culinary traditions head-on. This resulted in a kitchen disaster of epic proportions. Picture this: Sarah, attempting to make collard greens according to my mother's sacred recipe, somehow managed to set off the smoke alarm three times. The resulting culinary creation, while ambitious, resembled something more akin to a swampy, overcooked mess than the tender, flavorful greens my mother produced with effortless grace. The smoke alarm's insistent shriek became the soundtrack to a chaotic scene that involved frantic fanning, open windows, and a near-riot when my mother discovered her prized cast iron skillet covered in a mysterious, blackened substance. Sarah, though mortified, managed to salvage the situation with a surprisingly effective deployment of baking soda and a heartfelt apology. My mother, softened by Sarah's earnest attempt and the resulting chaotic humor, ultimately forgave her, offering a knowing smile and a muttered, "Well, honey, you've got spirit." The incident became a running family joke, a testament to the fact that even cultural clashes could be overcome with a healthy dose of laughter and fried chicken.

My attempts to integrate into Sarah's world proved equally challenging. Her family's Sunday brunch wasn't a casual affair involving greasy spoons and family chatter. Oh no, this was a meticulously planned event, more akin to a high-society gala than a casual meal. Imagine a pristine, white tablecloth, impossibly delicate china, and enough silverware to equip a small army. The conversation was as polished as the table setting, a carefully choreographed dance of polite small talk and sophisticated pronouncements about the merits of various investment portfolios. I, armed with my usual folksy humor and stories about my Uncle Earl's unfortunate encounter with a runaway pig, felt like a farm animal let loose in a crystal palace. My attempts at humor were met with tight-lipped smiles and subtle shifts in conversation, the unspoken message clear: "Please, try to fit in." I managed to survive the brunch without spilling anything on the exquisite tablecloth, a personal victory that I celebrated later with a well-deserved plate of greasy fried chicken from my mother's kitchen. The cultural divide was significant, yet the humor arising from these differences provided a common ground and a unique lens through which to navigate the relationship.

One memorable evening, we decided to take on the challenge of watching a movie together – a classic 90s rom-com that had both of our generations laughing. It's amazing how many cultural references were specific to this time – it was like a flashback, especially for me. The movie was punctuated by Sarah's confusion at certain slang terms, jokes and fashion choices, while I found myself patiently explaining the intricacies of early 90's hip-hop culture. The experience of trying to explain the phenomenon of parachute pants or the charm of a certain boy band brought another layer of hilarity to the encounter. The differences became the funny bits that were unique to our experiences, and our shared laughter made the experience a truly bonding moment.

Our attempts at navigating social events also proved hilarious. At a work Christmas party, Sarah encountered the bizarre world of office holiday games, including a particularly ludicrous rendition of "Pin the Tail on the Donkey" involving tiny Santa hats and a particularly grumpy-looking office mascot. I, meanwhile, had to endure Sarah's attempts at participating in a lively game of Spades, resulting in a disastrous hand that involved quite a bit of accidental card-slinging. This event became a source of endless amusement and strengthened the bond we were building through our shared experiences.

Another weekend brought a new adventure – Sarah's family's annual summer barbeque, a meticulously planned event involving croquet, elaborate cocktails, and a disturbing number of pastel-colored linens. My mother's contribution to the feast, a massive, flavorful pot of gumbo, clashed rather dramatically with the delicate cucumber sandwiches and quiche. The culture clash was not only food related; the conversations were as varied. Her family, composed of lawyers, doctors, and investment bankers, engaged in discussions about stocks, bonds, and international affairs while my family traded jokes about Uncle Earl's latest exploits and debated the merits of different BBQ sauces. The contrast created a hilarious juxtaposition, a comedic collision of cultures that made for an evening filled with awkward silences, surprised glances, and a healthy dose of laughter.

As weeks turned into months, we learned to appreciate the nuances of each other's cultures. I learned to appreciate the elegance of Sarah's world, while she, in turn, discovered the vibrant warmth and chaotic energy of mine. The cultural differences became less of a source of conflict and more of a unique spice in our relationship, adding flavor and humor to our journey. The cultural differences were the source of many humorous situations – imagine Sarah trying to navigate the complexities of a family reunion, where the prize for winning the family talent show was a lifetime supply of Aunt Gladys' famous sweet potato pie, which only she knows the secret recipe for. And there was the time when I attempted to explain the importance of soul food as a cornerstone of Black culture, only to be met with polite but bewildered expressions. These funny and often frustrating experiences underscored the challenges yet emphasized the importance of patience, tolerance, and love.

We learned that understanding each other wasn't about discarding our identities but about embracing our differences and celebrating our unique backgrounds. The humor in the incongruities made navigating those differences far more rewarding and engaging. The laughter, shared amidst the chaos of merging two such different worlds, became the glue that held us together, a testament to the enduring power of love in the face of cultural divides. And amidst all the misunderstandings, and the culinary calamities, we were finding a rhythm, a way to navigate this unusual family life with a shared sense of humor and a growing love that defied all odds. The 90s soundtrack to our lives, from hip hop to alternative rock, provided a nostalgic backdrop to our evolving relationship, a soundtrack that reflected the changes and the funny mishaps that became a part of our narrative. This journey was far from over, filled with more cultural clashes, more hilarious misunderstandings, and more opportunities to find humor in the face of adversity. But now, we faced it together, armed with laughter, patience, and a mutual respect for the richness of our different backgrounds.

The wedding planning process began, not with a gentle breeze of romance, but with a hurricane of conflicting opinions. Sarah, envisioning a rustic-chic affair with lavender accents and artisanal cheeses, found herself battling my mother's unwavering belief that a "proper" wedding required a gospel choir, a mountain of fried chicken, and enough collard greens to feed a small army. My mother, bless her heart, viewed wedding planning as a competition, a culinary Olympics where the ultimate prize was bragging rights for the most impressive spread. Sarah's attempts to introduce the concept of a "seated dinner" were met with incredulous stares and muttered comments about the importance of family-style servings, fostering a sense of communal togetherness.

Sarah's mother, bless her equally well-meaning heart, was a different breed of challenge. She envisioned a sophisticated affair, a refined gathering of esteemed guests, where the champagne flowed freely and the conversations were punctuated by cultured pronouncements on the merits of various art forms. This clashed wildly with my family's boisterous, almost chaotic, approach to celebrations. The mere suggestion of a formal seating chart sent my Aunt Gladys into a frenzy of anxieties, as the thought of separating feuding cousins risked igniting a family war. My Uncle Earl, ever the pragmatist, simply asked if they'd be serving enough moonshine to lubricate the inevitable conflicts.

The guest list itself became a battlefield. My family, a sprawling network of aunts, uncles, cousins, and second cousins twice removed, felt strongly that everyone should be included, no matter how distant the familial connection. Sarah's family, a more tightly knit group of professionals, preferred a more curated affair with only the closest family members and a select group of friends. The compromise, arrived at after a series of heated phone calls and tearful negotiations, was a guest list so extensive that it resembled a small-town census.

Then there was the matter of the music. Sarah's vision of a string quartet playing classical pieces was met with my family's demand for a live gospel choir, followed by a DJ spinning a mix of 90s hip-hop, R&B; and the latest dancehall hits. The thought of this eclectic mix of genres playing in the same venue threatened to create an auditory clash of epic proportions. We attempted a compromise, proposing a playlist that seamlessly transitioned from Bach to Biggie, a move that was met with bewildered expressions and much muttering. In the end, we hired both the string quartet and the gospel choir, creating a soundtrack as uniquely blended as our families.

The wedding attire became another source of comedic friction. Sarah, naturally, dreamt of a flowing, elegant gown. My mother, however, felt strongly that the bride should be adorned in traditional African attire, preferably something made of brightly colored kente cloth. This suggestion, though well-intentioned, was met with Sarah's polite but firm suggestion that she would stick to her original vision. The compromise involved incorporating elements of African-inspired design into the wedding decor instead – a concession my mother accepted after a carefully orchestrated campaign that involved the promise of multiple family-style meals featuring fried chicken and her signature collard greens.

The ceremony itself was a testament to our ability to blend two very different worlds. The string quartet played a beautiful rendition of "Ave Maria" as Sarah walked down the aisle, her dress the picture of classic elegance. As she approached the altar, however, the gospel choir launched into a soulful rendition of "This Little Light of Mine," bringing a powerful spiritual energy to the proceedings. The contrast was striking, but somehow, it worked. It felt uniquely 'us.' The exchange of vows was heartfelt and moving, a testament to the love that had brought us together despite the cultural differences.

The reception was even more eclectic. The wedding cake, a three-tiered masterpiece, was juxtaposed with a mountain of fried chicken and collard greens, a buffet representing the essence of both our families. The champagne flowed freely alongside gallons of sweet tea, and the guests mingled, navigating the differences with surprising ease and grace. My Uncle Earl, surprisingly, found himself deeply engaged in a conversation with Sarah's Aunt Mildred, two people you'd think had nothing in common. Their shared delight in a particularly spicy batch of hot sauce served as a common ground.

The dance floor was a whirlwind of activity. The string quartet's elegant melodies battled it out with the gospel choir's passionate vocals and the DJ's 90s hip hop beats; the dance floor itself became a kaleidoscope of styles, a reflection of our blended cultures. My family's exuberant line dancing clashed with Sarah's family's more restrained waltz, creating a hilarious collision of dance styles. Sarah's attempts to participate in the Electric Slide, while endearing, were punctuated by a certain lack of coordination that had everyone in stitches.

Despite the initial anxieties and the inevitable clashes, the wedding was a resounding success. It was a celebration not only of our love but also of the unique and wonderful differences that had brought our families together. The laughter, the shared experiences, the unexpected connections – all contributed to a day that was far more memorable and unique than anything we could have planned. The wedding, far from being a battleground, became a testament to the power of love to overcome cultural divides and forge a new path, a path that was paved with both laughter and tears, but ultimately led to a beautifully blended family, one that valued the rich tapestry of experiences and perspectives that each individual brought to the table.

The final dance, a slow waltz, found Sarah and me swaying to the gentle strains of the string quartet. As the music faded, we looked out at our families, a diverse group united by love, laughter, and a shared understanding that sometimes the most beautiful things come from unexpected collisions. The blend of cultures was not simply a compromise, it was a vibrant celebration, a testament to the power of merging different worlds and finding beauty in the clash of cultures. The wedding bells chimed not only the start of our marriage, but the beginning of a truly unique and hilarious family saga. It was a journey filled with challenges, yes, but challenges overcome with a shared sense of humor, a deep love, and an appreciation for the rich tapestry of our different worlds. The story, however, was far from over; it was merely the beginning of a whole new chapter filled with more cultural clashes, more hilarious misunderstandings, and more opportunities to find joy and laughter in the face of an ever-evolving, and endlessly entertaining, family dynamic.

Our honeymoon, a trip planned with the meticulous care only two people who'd just survived a wedding orchestrated by their combined families could muster, was booked to Jamaica. Sarah, ever the planner, had envisioned romantic sunsets, candlelit dinners, and leisurely strolls along pristine beaches. I, ever the pragmatist, had simply wanted a place with a decent rum punch and a reliable supply of jerk chicken. The 90s were in full swing, so naturally, our playlist consisted primarily of Boyz II Men, TLC, and a healthy dose of Brandy and Monica's "The Boy Is Mine," which, surprisingly, became our unofficial honeymoon anthem – a testament to our ability to find common ground even in musical tastes.

The first clash arrived even before we'd left the airport. Sarah, equipped with a meticulously researched itinerary that included snorkeling excursions, sunset cruises, and a visit to a local spice market, looked at my oversized duffel bag with suspicion. "That's all you're bringing?" she asked, eyebrows raised. My bag, in contrast to her perfectly coordinated luggage, contained an assortment of oversized t-shirts, several pairs of worn-out sneakers, a well-loved copy of "The Art of War" (because you never know when you might need a little Sun Tzu on your honeymoon), and a suspiciously large container of hot sauce.

The flight itself was a microcosm of our differences. Sarah settled into her seat with a copy of "Pride and Prejudice," lost in the world of Jane Austen. I, meanwhile, was happily engrossed in a game of Tetris on my Game Boy, my competitive spirit fueled by the desire to achieve the highest score on the notoriously challenging game. The juxtaposition of Jane Austen and Tetris was perhaps the perfect metaphor for our marriage – an unlikely but surprisingly harmonious blend of highbrow and lowbrow culture.

Our resort, a luxurious all-inclusive in Montego Bay, offered a stark contrast to my childhood memories of family vacations in the Catskills. Sarah, thrilled by the sheer opulence, was immediately enamored with the pristine beach, the turquoise waters, and the endless supply of cocktails. I, on the other hand, was captivated by the buffet, a seemingly endless array of delicious food that could rival my mother's culinary creations. The sheer quantity of food alone could spark a family-size feud.

The first real challenge emerged on our first full day. Sarah's meticulously planned snorkeling excursion, complete with high-tech snorkeling gear and a detailed marine life guide, was met with my utter lack of enthusiasm for aquatic activities. The sight of my slightly panicked face as I was submerged beneath the water, frantically trying to remember which way was up, had Sarah struggling to keep a straight face. The sight of me, clinging to a life raft for dear life, my snorkel hanging precariously from my ear, was apparently quite amusing.

The evenings were equally eventful. Sarah's romantic dinners, featuring candlelight, fine wine, and subtle background music, were often interrupted by my sudden urges to sample every local delicacy. My obsession with jerk chicken, seasoned with a liberal dose of my own hot sauce, was a constant source of amusement and, at times, slight concern to Sarah. Sarah's attempts to introduce me to the finer points of Jamaican cuisine, including escovitch fish and callaloo soup, were met with an enthusiastic acceptance, followed by a hasty dash to the nearest bathroom due to my mild (but entirely predictable) reaction to unfamiliar spices.

Our attempts at romantic walks along the beach were equally hilarious. Sarah, a picture of grace and elegance, carefully navigated the sand, her steps measured and deliberate. I, however, frequently tripped over my own feet, my clumsiness underscored by my efforts to maintain a smooth, suave demeanor. This usually involved much stumbling, laughter, and an almost inevitable fall into the sand.

We attempted to partake in activities that were somewhat of a compromise. Sarah's desire for cultural immersion led to a visit to a local market, which I initially viewed as an opportunity to purchase more hot sauce. I inadvertently, however, found myself fascinated by the vibrant colors, the exotic aromas, and the lively interactions among the vendors. Sarah, amused by my sudden enthusiasm, indulged my obsession with procuring every variety of hot sauce imaginable, even helping me haggle with a particularly stubborn vendor. This exchange became a highlight of our trip, a hilarious reminder that even the most unexpected experiences can lead to shared joy and laughter.

One evening, under the shimmering moonlight, as we sat on our balcony sipping cocktails, a rather profound conversation arose. Sarah confessed to feeling a bit overwhelmed by the sheer intensity of my family. I, in turn, admitted to being slightly intimidated by her refined sensibilities and her preference for a perfectly organized schedule. The conversation, although initially laced with anxieties and self-doubts, eventually led to a shared understanding. We both acknowledged that our differences were part of what made us a unique and fascinating pair.

The last day of our honeymoon, we spent it simply relaxing by the pool. No meticulously planned excursions, no cultural immersion, just us, soaking up the sun and enjoying each other's company. As we looked back at our honeymoon, it wasn't the idyllic romantic getaway Sarah had envisioned, nor was it the jerk-chicken-fueled adventure I'd secretly hoped for. It was something entirely different, something unique and utterly hilarious. It was a chaotic, beautiful, perfectly imperfect reflection of our relationship – a blend of highbrow and lowbrow, of meticulous planning and happy accidents, of controlled chaos and unexpected joy. Our honeymoon was not only the beginning of our married life; it was a comedic prelude to the family saga to come.

Chapter 2: Family Feuds and Funerals

Thanksgiving. The word itself conjured images of warmth, family, and copious amounts of food. My vision, however, was considerably less idyllic. It involved a clash of cultures, a culinary catastrophe of epic proportions, and the distinct possibility of a family feud that would make the Hatfields and McCoys look like a friendly bridge club.

Sarah, bless her organized heart, had approached our first Thanksgiving as a blended family with the same meticulous planning she'd applied to our honeymoon. She'd drawn up a detailed schedule, a color-coded chart outlining every element of the day, from the precise timing of the turkey's arrival in the oven to the optimal temperature for the cranberry sauce. My mother, bless her chaotic heart, had approached it with a hearty dose of "winging it," armed with her secret weapon: a recipe for sweet potato casserole that involved an alarming amount of marshmallows.

The first sign of trouble emerged during the grocery shopping. Sarah, clutching her meticulously compiled shopping list, navigated the aisles with the precision of a seasoned surgeon. I, on the other hand, was captivated by a mountain of brightly colored Jell-O molds, a nostalgic reminder of my childhood Thanksgivings. Sarah's delicate eyebrow arched in disapproval when I insisted on purchasing three different flavors – lime, cherry, and the pièce de résistance, a particularly alarming shade of green that we'd later come to term "Nuclear Green."

The preparation of the Thanksgiving feast was, to put it mildly, chaotic. Sarah's pristine kitchen, normally a sanctuary of order and cleanliness, quickly descended into organized chaos. Pots and pans clattered, spices flew, and the aroma of roasting turkey mingled with the surprisingly potent odor of Sarah's experimental cranberry sauce (a combination of pomegranate juice and ginger that smelled suspiciously like cough medicine). My mother, meanwhile, presided over the sweet potato casserole like a benevolent dictator, occasionally pausing her marshmallow-application process to offer unsolicited advice on the proper way to carve a turkey.

The actual carving of the turkey proved to be another source of contention. Sarah, armed with her carving set and a copy of "The Joy of Cooking," performed the task with surgical precision. My mother, however, approached it with the gusto of a seasoned lumberjack, wielding her kitchen knife with reckless abandon. The result was a somewhat mangled, but undeniably delicious, turkey.

The dinner itself was a symphony of culinary clashes. Sarah's elegant presentation, featuring individually plated servings of roasted vegetables and her experimental cranberry sauce, was met with my mother's hearty heaping of mashed potatoes, topped with gravy that was, to be kind, a bit runny. The aforementioned Jell-O molds made a surprisingly prominent appearance, their vibrant hues a stark contrast to the traditional earth tones of the other dishes. The juxtaposition of Sarah's sophisticated palate and my mother's down-home cooking was, to put it mildly, explosive.

Conversation was equally fraught with tension. Sarah's well-meaning attempts at polite conversation were constantly interrupted by my mother's booming laughter and unsolicited commentary on Sarah's choice of clothing ("That's a lovely sweater, dear, though I think a touch more color would suit your complexion"). My attempts to mediate between the two ended up with me caught in a crossfire of conflicting opinions, forced to play the role of the hapless peacemaker.

The children, bless their innocent hearts, seemed entirely unfazed by the simmering tension. They were preoccupied with their own form of Thanksgiving chaos, engaging in a food fight of epic proportions that involved mashed potatoes, cranberry sauce, and, of course, that nuclear green Jell-O. The aftermath was a scene of sticky fingers, stained clothing, and a general sense of joyful pandemonium.

The evening concluded with a collective sense of exhaustion and a surprising amount of laughter. We'd somehow survived our first Thanksgiving as a blended family, emerging from the ordeal with a newfound appreciation for each other's quirks and a shared understanding of the absurdities of family dynamics. While the Thanksgiving feast itself was a culinary disaster and social minefield, the chaotic energy, the laughter, and the shared experience helped forge a bond that was both unique and incredibly strong.

The next morning, as I surveyed the kitchen, littered with remnants of the Thanksgiving feast, a sense of bittersweet nostalgia washed over me. The disaster had been monumental, a true testament to the challenges of blending two vastly different families. But somewhere amid the culinary chaos and the family feuds, something magical had happened. We had created our own Thanksgiving tradition, a unique blend of cultures and personalities, a celebration of our differences and the unexpected joy that arose from the clash. The memory of that first Thanksgiving, a chaotic and hilarious culmination of culinary mishaps and family drama, became a cherished symbol of our blended family's resilience and enduring bond. It was a reminder that sometimes, the most memorable gatherings aren't the ones flawlessly executed, but those where the imperfections and laughter create the strongest and most enduring memories. The following years' Thanksgivings were still eventful, but the first one remained the legendary benchmark, the one against which all subsequent celebrations would be measured. It was the Thanksgiving that taught us that family, however unconventional, could always find a way to come together, even if it involved a lot of gravy, a significant amount of Jell-O, and a healthy dose of good-natured chaos. The 90s aesthetic was alive and well in our unconventional Thanksgiving, from the chunky sweaters to the plentiful gravy boats, and the resulting photographic evidence was, to put it mildly, priceless. It was a snapshot of a family finding its way, one culinary catastrophe and hilarious misunderstanding at a time. And, as any good sitcom would attest, the messy situations always made for the best stories. The subsequent years brought their own brand of Thanksgiving mayhem, but none ever quite matched the glorious, chaotic brilliance of that first, unforgettable Thanksgiving. The legacy of the "Nuclear Green" Jell-O alone ensured its place in family folklore, a testament to the lasting power of laughter in the face of culinary disaster. The family photos, slightly blurry and bursting with the energy of the day, captured more than just a holiday gathering; they immortalized the spirit of our unconventional family, forever bound together by a shared experience, a perfectly imperfect Thanksgiving, and a lifetime's worth of hilarious anecdotes.

Christmas. The very word should evoke images of twinkling lights, crackling fireplaces, and the sweet scent of pine needles. Instead, it conjured up visions of a potential three-alarm family fire – the kind fueled not by flames, but by clashing holiday traditions, wildly different gift-giving philosophies, and a decorating dispute that threatened to rival the Cold War.

Sarah, ever the planner, had approached Christmas with her usual military-grade precision. A detailed schedule, complete with color-coded timelines for wrapping presents, baking cookies, and decorating the tree, was already in effect weeks before the big day. My mother, on the other hand, approached the holidays with the same "winging it" approach she employed during Thanksgiving, her only preparation being the acquisition of an industrial-sized tub of peppermint bark and a questionable collection of vintage Christmas ornaments acquired from various garage sales over the years. One of these ornaments, a ceramic Santa inexplicably wearing roller skates, was already causing a mild family crisis.

The first skirmish erupted over the Christmas tree. Sarah envisioned a perfectly symmetrical Douglas fir, adorned with elegant, minimalist decorations – think frosted glass balls, tasteful silver ribbons, and perhaps a scattering of pinecones for a touch of rustic charm. My mother, however, had other plans. Her vision of a Christmas tree involved maximum tinsel, a rainbow assortment of mismatched ornaments (including the roller-skating Santa), and enough twinkling lights to rival a small airport runway. The result was a tree that looked like a festive explosion in a craft store, a glorious clash of styles that reflected the eclectic mix of our family. The ensuing debate could have powered a small city with its sheer volume of conflicting opinions and heartfelt pleas. Sarah argued for restraint, order, and a certain level of sophistication; my mother, armed with the sheer force of her personality and an alarming amount of leftover Christmas garland from previous years, championed maximalism, nostalgia, and, frankly, a little bit of festive chaos. I found myself once again caught in the middle, desperately attempting to negotiate a peace treaty between two opposing armies, each determined to defend their decorating vision.

Gift-giving presented another battlefield. Sarah favored practical gifts, thoughtfully chosen and beautifully wrapped. Her presents were a testament to her thoughtful nature, each one imbued with a level of personal consideration that left no one wanting. My mother, however, believed in the power of the surprise, the more extravagant, the better. Her gifts ranged from wildly impractical novelty items to slightly questionable second-hand treasures from her extensive collection of garage sale finds. This resulted in a plethora of gifts that were equal parts hilarious and confusing. The children, naturally, were overjoyed by the sheer abundance, but the adults found themselves navigating a minefield of potential offense. One particularly awkward moment involved Sarah's carefully curated gift of a high-end cashmere sweater being overshadowed by my mother's gift of a life-size inflatable snowman that somehow managed to deflate within minutes of being set up.

Religious observance added another layer of complexity. Sarah's family celebrated Christmas in a quiet, contemplative manner, emphasizing the spiritual aspects of the holiday. My family, on the other hand, embraced a more boisterous approach, with an emphasis on family gatherings, gift-giving, and copious amounts of food. This resulted in a tension-filled Christmas Eve that showcased both approaches. The quiet, candlelit service Sarah's family preferred was followed by my mother's insistence on a raucous family singalong, complete with slightly off-key carols and an impromptu dance-off fueled by spiked eggnog. This made Sarah's elegant, candlelit Christmas Eve dinner look like a scene out of a high-society drama compared to the cheerful, slightly chaotic celebration that followed. The resulting blend was, to say the least, unique – a fascinating collision of quiet reflection and exuberant celebration. The children, however, seemed thoroughly unfazed by the contrast, happily flitting between both family gatherings, their faces bright with the joyous energy of the holidays.

The Christmas meal itself was a culinary masterpiece of contrasts. Sarah's meticulously crafted Christmas dinner, a symphony of roasted meats, delicate vegetables, and elegant desserts, was juxtaposed with my mother's hearty, comfort-food approach – a mountain of mashed potatoes, a colossal ham, and an abundance of those infamous sweet potato casseroles (this time, with even more marshmallows). The resulting feast was a testament to the diversity of our family, a glorious clash of culinary styles that left everyone completely satisfied, albeit slightly overwhelmed.

The 90s aesthetic, meanwhile, played a crucial role in the festive chaos. From the gaudy Christmas sweaters to the abundance of tinsel and the abundance of brightly colored ornaments, the holiday decorations themselves were a snapshot of the era. And those decorations clashed with Sarah's more minimalist décor, creating a decorating collision that was both beautiful and slightly jarring in its contrast. The family photos from that Christmas, slightly blurry and bursting with the energy of the day, captured more than just a holiday gathering. They immortalized the spirit of our unconventional family, forever bound together by a shared experience, a perfectly imperfect Christmas, and a lifetime's worth of hilarious anecdotes. The legacy of the roller-skating Santa alone was enough to ensure its place in family folklore, a testament to the lasting power of laughter in the face of holiday madness. The memories of that first Christmas, as a blended family, are a testament to the enduring strength of love, acceptance, and the hilarious chaos that often comes with family. We learned that Christmas, like life itself, is not about perfection but about embracing the laughter, the imperfections, and the sheer joy of being together, even if it meant navigating a minefield of clashing traditions and questionable gift choices. And, as any good sitcom would attest, the messy situations always made for the best stories. The subsequent years brought their own brand of Christmas mayhem, but none ever quite matched the glorious, chaotic brilliance of that first, unforgettable Christmas. The blend of high-society elegance and down-home charm, of carefully crafted gifts and wildly impractical surprises, of contemplative quietude and joyful exuberance, created a Christmas experience that was uniquely ours – a blend that showcased our diverse family and traditions. The resulting memories are a source of continuous laughter and a heartwarming reminder of the true meaning of family. We learned to accept each other's differences, to celebrate our unique styles, and to find joy in the unexpected chaos of it all. And, most importantly, we discovered that the most beautiful Christmas memories are the ones crafted not by perfection but by laughter, love, and a little bit of good-natured holiday pandemonium.

The post-Christmas lull was, surprisingly, relatively peaceful. The roller-skating Santa had been carefully packed away (after a near-fatal incident involving a rogue cat and a strategically placed extension cord), and a fragile truce had been established between Sarah's minimalist sensibilities and my mother's maximalist tendencies. We were all slightly exhausted, but content, the afterglow of the holiday season still warming our hearts. Then came the news.

It wasn't a dramatic reveal, no fainting couches or melodramatic pronouncements. It was a quiet announcement, made over a lukewarm cup of coffee one particularly dreary January morning. Sarah, looking a little pale but undeniably radiant, simply stated, "I'm pregnant."

The silence that followed was deafening. My mother, mid-bite of a particularly buttery biscuit, froze. The biscuit, suspended halfway between plate and mouth, seemed to hang in the air, a culinary monument to stunned silence. I, meanwhile, felt a wave of dizziness wash over me, the coffee suddenly tasting decidedly less lukewarm and more like battery acid.

Sarah's calm demeanor didn't quite mask the tremor in her voice. It wasn't just the pregnancy itself, but the sheer weight of expectation from both sides of the family that hung heavily in the air. This wasn't just another addition to our already unconventional family dynamic, it was a seismic shift, threatening to upend an already precarious balance. The implications were staggering, and the comic potential, I realised with a grim sense of foreboding, was immense.

My mother, ever the pragmatist (when it suited her), was the first to recover. "Well, honey," she announced, her voice surprisingly steady, "that's just wonderful! Although," she added, a mischievous glint in her eye, "I do hope it's a girl. We need another woman in this family who can stand up to your father." She winked at Sarah, seemingly oblivious to the potentially incendiary nature of her statement. I braced myself. This was going to be a long year.

Sarah, however, took the comment in stride. "Mom," she said, with a gentle but firm tone that suggested years of experience navigating my mother's pronouncements, "I'm sure the baby will be perfect, regardless of gender." The subtle undercurrent of passive aggression was unmistakable.

My reaction was more visceral. I felt a mixture of excitement, terror, and overwhelming confusion. The practicalities alone seemed insurmountable. How would we manage another child with our already chaotic schedules? How would we navigate the clashing parenting styles? And most importantly, how would we handle the fallout from both sets of grandparents?

My mother's family, a boisterous clan from the rural south, were already prone to excessive displays of affection and unsolicited advice. Their reaction was predictable. A flurry of phone calls followed, punctuated by squeals of delight, copious amounts of Southern cooking, and enough unsolicited baby advice to fill a small library. My mother dispatched a team of aunts and cousins to take over the housework and enforce a strict diet of healthy foods (which Sarah managed to sneakily undermine by hiding jars of Nutella in strategic locations throughout the house).

Sarah's family, a more reserved bunch from upstate New York, approached the news with a carefully curated mixture of polite enthusiasm and thinly veiled concern. They sent carefully chosen gifts – organic baby clothes, educational toys, and a hefty supply of high-end baby formula – all meticulously wrapped in understated packaging. Their concern, however, was subtle but present, laced with concern about cultural differences and potential challenges. Subtle comments about the importance of a stable upbringing and the nuances of parenting in a multicultural family punctuated their well-wishes.

The ensuing months were a dizzying blend of doctor's appointments, ultrasound scans, and family gatherings that could only be described as "intense." My mother, convinced that she was the only one qualified to provide childcare advice, launched a relentless campaign of unsolicited tips that ranged from bizarre home remedies to questionable superstitions. Sarah, with her meticulous planning and research, countered with evidence-based childcare strategies and a mountain of parenting books. I found myself once again caught in the middle, refereeing arguments about swaddling techniques, sleep training methods, and the merits of organic baby food versus homemade purees.

The differing expectations about gender roles further complicated matters. My mother envisioned a future where the new baby would be constantly surrounded by a doting army of aunts, uncles, and cousins, showering the child with love, attention, and copious amounts of Southern-style hospitality. Sarah, meanwhile, envisioned a balanced approach, with a fair distribution of childcare responsibilities between me and herself, emphasizing independence and self-sufficiency. The resulting clashes were, to say the least, entertaining.

The cultural differences between both sets of grandparents added another layer of comedic tension. My mother's family, with their boisterous traditions and unconventional approach to childcare, clashed constantly with Sarah's parents' more reserved, structured parenting style. Visits from the grandparents invariably ended in a flurry of good-natured arguments, hilarious misunderstandings, and a mountain of dirty dishes.

The baby shower itself was a masterclass in cultural fusion. Sarah's family organized a sophisticated, elegant affair, complete with a champagne toast and a carefully curated selection of hors d'oeuvres. My mother, however, decided to throw a separate party, a raucous celebration that involved live music, a pig roast, and enough homemade casseroles to feed a small army. The resulting events showcased a striking juxtaposition of elegance and down-home charm. The photos, once again, would be testament to the absurdity of it all.

The arrival of the baby, a healthy bouncing girl (much to my mother's delight), did little to calm the waters. The clashing parenting styles persisted, the unsolicited advice continued, and the cultural differences only seemed to amplify. But amidst the chaos, laughter echoed, a constant soundtrack to our unconventional family life. The journey of parenthood, as we were quickly discovering, was far from perfect, but it was undeniably hilarious – a testament to the enduring power of love, resilience, and the occasional good-natured family feud. And somewhere, amidst the chaos, amidst the clashing parenting philosophies and wildly divergent family traditions, we were forging our own unique brand of family, one laugh at a time. The roller-skating Santa was long forgotten, but this new chapter, this new adventure, was already shaping up to be the most memorable story yet. The comedic potential was simply endless.

The arrival of Aunt Mildred, a woman whose existence had been previously relegated to dusty family photo albums and whispered anecdotes, threw a wrench into the already finely tuned chaos of our lives. She materialized on our doorstep one blustery March afternoon, a whirlwind of floral print, oversized sunglasses, and a suitcase overflowing with enough vintage Tupperware to supply a small army. Aunt Mildred, it turned out, was my mother's estranged sister, a woman who, according to family legend, had run off to join a travelling circus in her youth and hadn't been seen since.

My mother's reaction was a bizarre mix of shock, delight, and a deep-seated sense of unease. She greeted Aunt Mildred with a shriek of pure joy, then immediately began interrogating her about the whereabouts of a priceless antique tea set that had mysteriously vanished decades ago. Sarah, ever the pragmatist, simply offered Aunt Mildred a cup of tea and a sympathetic ear, sensing that this reunion was going to be anything but smooth sailing. I, however, was already mentally composing the stand-up routine this unexpected guest was going to provide.

Aunt Mildred, it soon became apparent, was a force of nature. She possessed an encyclopedic knowledge of obscure family gossip, a penchant for dramatic storytelling, and a wardrobe that could rival a Broadway costume designer's workshop. Her arrival instantly reignited long-dormant family feuds, dredging up old grievances and resurrecting forgotten rivalries. My mother's carefully constructed truce with Sarah crumbled under the onslaught of Aunt Mildred's tales of family scandals and long-forgotten betrayals.

The stories, it turned out, were legendary. There was the infamous incident involving Uncle Edgar, a prize-winning pig, and a runaway hay baler, a tale Aunt Mildred recounted with such gusto that Sarah nearly choked on her tea. Then there was the saga of Great-Aunt Beatrice, a woman who apparently once challenged a reigning Miss America to a pie-eating contest, resulting in a chaotic showdown involving flour bombs and a broken tiara. Each story, no matter how outlandish, was delivered with such conviction and flair that it was impossible to dismiss them as mere exaggerations.

Sarah's family, already wary of our family's boisterous nature, found themselves completely out of their depth. Aunt Mildred's unconventional views on parenting, which involved everything from letting the baby sleep in a hammock suspended from the ceiling to feeding it a diet of exclusively organic kale smoothies (a concept that horrified my mother), created friction between her and Sarah's parents. Their attempts at polite conversation invariably devolved into a series of awkward silences punctuated by the occasional strained chuckle.

Meanwhile, my mother, seizing the opportunity to reclaim the family narrative, launched her own counter-offensive, armed with a photo album filled with embarrassing childhood pictures and a seemingly endless supply of anecdotes that painted Aunt Mildred in a less-than-flattering light. The two women, locked in a battle of wits and familial one-upmanship, provided an endless stream of comedic fodder. Their skirmishes became legendary, a daily soap opera played out in our living room, complete with dramatic pronouncements, whispered accusations, and the occasional thrown cushion.

Adding to the already complex family dynamics was the revelation of a long-lost family secret, one that had been carefully concealed for generations. Aunt Mildred, it turned out, was not only my mother's estranged sister but also the key to unlocking a decades-old mystery involving a missing inheritance and a forged will. This revelation sent shockwaves through the family, further exacerbating existing tensions and introducing new layers of conflict.

The search for the missing inheritance became a chaotic scavenger hunt, leading us on a wild goose chase across town, from dusty attics filled with forgotten treasures to forgotten family businesses that hadn't seen action in a century. Aunt Mildred, armed with cryptic clues and a tattered map, led the charge, dragging the rest of the family in her wake. It was pure comedic mayhem.

My mother, spurred on by the prospect of financial gain, teamed up with Aunt Mildred, forming an unlikely alliance that threatened to upend the fragile peace Sarah had carefully constructed. Sarah, ever the mediator, attempted to maintain order, but found herself constantly battling the forces of family chaos, dodging flying teacups and navigating the minefield of familial secrets.

The climax of the inheritance hunt unfolded during a particularly chaotic family dinner, one where Aunt Mildred, in a fit of theatrical flair, revealed the location of the hidden treasure: a dusty, forgotten strongbox hidden beneath the floorboards of my great-grandmother's ancestral home. The ensuing scramble for the box was a sight to behold, a whirlwind of frantic family members tumbling over furniture and each other, vying for possession of what turned out to be a collection of slightly moth-eaten antique doilies and a stack of love letters written in a language none of us understood.

The disappointment was palpable, but the sheer absurdity of it all was undeniably hilarious. We were left, not with a fortune, but with a renewed appreciation for our eccentric family, their deeply rooted quirks, and the sheer comedic value of a good family feud. Aunt Mildred's unexpected visit may have stirred up trouble, but it also reminded us of the strange, wonderful bond that held us together, a bond cemented by shared laughter, family secrets, and the occasional well-aimed cushion. It was, in its own chaotic way, a beautiful thing. The roller-skating Santa, the clashing parenting styles, the baby – they all paled in comparison to the sheer, unadulterated entertainment provided by Aunt Mildred's temporary but indelible mark on our lives. The comedic potential, I realized, had only just begun to blossom. This wasn't just a family; it was a comedic masterpiece in the making. And I, the unwitting narrator, was front row center. The story of our unconventional family was far from over, and each new chapter promised more laughter, more chaos, and more unforgettable moments. The next family gathering, I thought with a shudder and a smile, would be… interesting.

The arrival of our little bundle of joy, a cherubic, gurgling human being named – in a moment of parental weakness – "Zahara," (a name that, let's just say, didn't exactly scream "Nineties," but what did we know? We were knee-deep in disposable diapers and sleep deprivation.) was like dropping a glitter bomb into an already chaotic family dynamic. It was glorious, messy, and utterly unpredictable. Picture this: a tiny human, swathed in a pastel-colored onesie adorned with cartoon dinosaurs (because, naturally, that's what all cool 90s babies wore), amidst a clash of parenting styles that were as different as night and day.

My approach to fatherhood, heavily influenced by my own upbringing, involved a healthy dose of laissez-faire. Let the kid cry it out, I figured. A little tough love never hurt anybody. Sarah, on the other hand, was a devotee of the "attachment parenting" movement, a philosophy that seemed to involve constant skin-to-skin contact, breastfeeding on demand (a demand that never seemed to cease), and an arsenal of baby carriers that rivaled a small-scale military operation. The result was a constant tug-of-war over Zahara's well-being, a battle fought with pacifiers, burp cloths, and the occasional tear-stained onesie.

Our families, already brimming with dysfunction, reacted to Zahara's arrival with the expected flair. My mother, convinced that every baby needed a daily dose of cod liver oil and a stern talking-to, viewed Sarah's gentle parenting style with a mixture of suspicion and open disdain. Sarah's parents, meanwhile, were horrified by my mother's apparent lack of maternal concern. They whispered anxieties about my mother's "old-fashioned methods" while secretly wondering if cod liver oil was, in fact, some kind of sinister, 90s-era voodoo potion.

Aunt Mildred, ever the instigator, seized the opportunity to weigh in on the matter, offering unsolicited advice on everything from babywearing techniques to the supposed benefits of homeopathic remedies (a claim I found particularly amusing, given her past association with a traveling circus – perhaps they had a travelling homeopath?). Her arrival, with its assortment of questionable herbal tinctures and an ancient, slightly moldy baby sling, caused Sarah's already stressed mother to declare, "I'm having a meltdown, and I'm taking the whole darn family with me!"

The resulting family gatherings were a masterclass in comedic chaos. Imagine a Thanksgiving dinner, but instead of a peaceful gathering of loved ones, picture a scene straight out of a Three Stooges movie. There were heated debates on the merits of cloth versus disposable diapers, fierce arguments over sleep training techniques, and whispered conspiracy theories about the potential dangers of commercial baby food. And throughout it all, little Zahara, seemingly oblivious to the maelstrom of parental conflict, continued to gurgle and drool, a tiny, innocent observer in the midst of the storm.

The 90s backdrop to all this only amplified the absurdity. Think oversized tracksuits, neon-colored toys, and an unending stream of grunge music, which somehow managed to blend seamlessly with the cacophony of family squabbles and the rhythmic sounds of a baby's cries. Sarah's parents, clinging desperately to the era's fleeting fashion trends, were constantly sporting clothes that clashed violently with the overall aesthetic of the house. My mother, firmly rooted in the past, seemed determined to raise Zahara in a pre-grunge world, which occasionally involved pulling out vintage dresses from her closet and attempting to dress the baby in them.

One particularly memorable incident involved a family game night. We'd decided on a relatively sedate game of Scrabble, hoping to find some semblance of peace and quiet. This plan, naturally, backfired spectacularly. Aunt Mildred, fueled by an inexplicable caffeine addiction and a misplaced sense of competitive spirit, cheated relentlessly. My mother, armed with a dictionary and a burning desire to win, countered with equally aggressive tactics. The game ended in a flurry of accusations, overturned Scrabble tiles, and a traumatized toddler who was crying less from hunger and more from the sheer volume of adult yelling.

Adding fuel to the fire was the constant stream of unsolicited advice from well-meaning (and not-so-well-meaning) relatives. Friends and family alike felt compelled to share their personal parenting expertise, from dubious home remedies to completely outdated child-rearing philosophies. The sheer volume of conflicting information was enough to drive even the most seasoned parent to the brink of madness.

One particularly well-meaning but utterly clueless neighbour suggested we try "spooking" Zahara to sleep by making scary noises. My mother, seeing this as an opportunity to teach a bit of old-fashioned discipline (or perhaps to have some fun at our expense), was all too eager to comply. This resulted in a highly entertaining (for us, slightly terrifying for Zahara) fifteen-minute performance of exaggerated goblin sounds and menacing cackles. Zahara, initially startled, eventually started laughing hysterically – probably finding the absurdity of the situation as comical as we did.

But amidst all the chaos, there were moments of genuine connection. The shared exhaustion of sleepless nights forged a bond between Sarah and me, a deeper understanding that transcended the usual parental squabbles. The sheer absurdity of the situation often dissolved into fits of laughter, a shared escape from the mounting pressures of parenthood. My mother, despite her initially skeptical attitude, displayed moments of surprising tenderness towards Zahara, showing a side of her that we rarely saw before. Even Sarah's initially apprehensive parents began to relax and enjoy some moments of (carefully curated) family fun.

The nineties – with their unique blend of economic boom and cultural anxieties – provided a fitting backdrop for our ever-evolving family. The decade's eclectic mix of fashion, music and cultural shifts played a pivotal role in shaping our family's comedic story, weaving itself seamlessly into the fabric of our everyday lives. From the slap bracelets and Tamagotchis to the ubiquitous boombox playing a soundtrack of grunge anthems, the nineties were present in every corner of our lives, making the whole experience even more hilariously unforgettable.

Through the sleepless nights, the chaotic family gatherings, and the never-ending stream of parenting advice, one thing remained constant: the underlying love that bound our family together, a love that was tested, challenged, and often stretched to its limits but always somehow persevered. As Zahara's first wobbly steps echoed through the house, mirroring the stumbling, often chaotic progress of our blended family, we realised that we were creating a unique and ultimately hilarious story, one that continues to unfold, one chapter – and one comedic stumble – at a time. The rollercoaster of parenthood, set against the backdrop of a truly unconventional family, was far from over; in fact, it was just beginning to gather speed.

Chapter 3: Bridging the Gap

Our attempts at cultural immersion began, predictably, with a disaster. Sarah, bless her ambitious heart, decided we should have a "soul food" dinner. Now, I'm a connoisseur of soul food, raised on my mama's legendary fried chicken and collard greens. Sarah, however, had gleaned her knowledge from a Betty Crocker cookbook and a brief stint watching a cooking show hosted by a celebrity chef whose understanding of Southern cuisine seemed limited to using the word "y'all" liberally.

The results were... interesting. Picture this: a pale imitation of macaroni and cheese, the texture somewhere between glue and rubber; collard greens that had clearly never seen a pot of ham hock; and fried chicken that looked suspiciously like it had been battered in plaster of Paris. The aroma, a bizarre concoction of burnt sugar and despair, hung heavy in the air.

Sarah, ever the optimist, beamed at her culinary creation, declaring it a "delicious fusion of flavors." I, on the other hand, choked down a bite, my face betraying my inner turmoil. My mother, ever the blunt instrument, declared it "an insult to the very spirit of soul food." The ensuing conversation, or rather, a series of increasingly strained apologies and carefully veiled insults, somehow involved a heated debate about the proper technique for peeling sweet potatoes.

Undeterred, Sarah decided to return the favor. She planned a "classic American dinner," which turned out to be a bizarre interpretation of Thanksgiving, complete with cranberry sauce that had the consistency of jelly and a turkey that was both dry and somehow simultaneously rubbery. My family, raised on more robust Southern traditions, treated this meal with the same level of bemusement as the first. The high point of the evening was my Uncle Earl's attempt to sneak a whole can of cranberry sauce into his pocket, a move he only abandoned after Aunt Mildred loudly declared that she would inform his wife.

Our attempts at cultural exchange extended beyond the culinary realm. Sarah decided we should learn a new language. Her choice? Mandarin. This made as much sense as a fish riding a bicycle, but Sarah, convinced that multilingualism was the key to marital bliss, persevered. We signed up for a weekend language course, only to discover that our combined aptitude for Mandarin was about as sharp as a marshmallow.

Our instructor, a patient but increasingly weary woman named Ms. Chen, spent the entire weekend trying to coax comprehensible sounds from us. Sarah's attempts sounded like a series of strangled coughs, while mine were more akin to a confused chimpanzee trying to imitate human speech. By the end of the weekend, we'd managed to learn the words for "hello," "goodbye," and "I need a large glass of wine."

Undeterred, we continued our pursuit of cultural understanding in other ways. Sarah attempted to teach me the art of pottery, an activity I approached with all the grace of a bull in a china shop. The results were predictably messy, resulting in a collection of lopsided mugs and a near-miss catastrophe involving a flying clay shard and my left eyebrow.

I, in turn, introduced Sarah to the joys of rhythm and blues. Or rather, I attempted to. Sarah, who preferred the smoother sounds of adult contemporary, initially struggled with the rawness and soulful grit of the music. I tried to explain the cultural significance of the music to her, the history and emotional depth behind the blues, but she remained unconvinced, preferring instead the soothing tones of her favorite smooth jazz artist.

One evening, in a moment of playful mischief, I decided to introduce Sarah to the wonderful world of gospel music. This involved a trip to a local church, a place where the level of enthusiasm was only matched by the volume of the singing. Sarah, initially apprehensive, found herself swept away by the music, laughing and singing along with the congregation. It was a moment of unexpected connection, a realization that music could transcend cultural divides.

Throughout this cross-cultural adventure, there were moments of genuine connection alongside the hilarious mishaps. We both discovered that cultural understanding was a journey, not a destination. The path was fraught with pitfalls – burnt collard greens, lopsided mugs, and attempts at Mandarin that sounded more like a cat fight – but the shared laughter and understanding that emerged from these experiences were far more valuable than anything we could have learned from a textbook or a cooking show.

Our efforts to bridge the cultural gap sometimes felt like we were attempting to build a bridge out of marshmallows and rubber bands, but it was that very process, filled with laughter and unexpected moments of genuine connection, that strengthened our bond.

The family dynamics, already volatile, reached new levels of absurdity. Sarah's parents, appalled by my mother's unorthodox methods of parenting, now found themselves facing new challenges: understanding a completely different culture and the resulting cultural clashes between both families. This led to some truly unforgettable dinners, where conversation topics veered from the pros and cons of different parenting styles to the finer points of Southern etiquette and the relative merits of different types of gravy.

My mother, however, continued her campaign of cultural indoctrination. She attempted to teach Sarah to play dominoes, a game Sarah found utterly baffling. She insisted Sarah learn to make biscuits from scratch, resulting in a disastrous baking attempt that involved a significant quantity of flour dust and a near-riot involving the kitchen mixer. My mother also took it upon herself to teach Sarah the art of storytelling, a skill Sarah possessed in abundance, and the outcome was a hilarious comparison of family traditions and anecdotes that kept everyone entertained for hours.

The contrast between our two families was sometimes jarring, a collision of personalities and traditions that occasionally threatened to erupt into a full-blown family feud. However, the undercurrent of affection and mutual respect always seemed to prevail. It was during this phase that we began to understand that bridging the gap wasn't about erasing our differences but about celebrating and respecting them.

Our efforts to understand each other's cultures were often met with hilarious miscommunications, leading to more misunderstandings and awkward situations than we could have ever imagined. But in those mishaps, a deeper bond formed. We learned that true connection wasn't about seamless cultural integration but about embracing the differences and finding laughter in the journey.

This chapter was a chaotic tapestry of cultural missteps and unexpected connections. It was a journey of learning and acceptance, filled with more laughter than we could have ever anticipated. It was a testament to the resilience of love and the enduring power of humor in the face of overwhelming cultural differences. And it was just the beginning. The story of our blended family, a chaotic blend of two vastly different cultures, was far from over. It was only just beginning to unfold, one hilarious misunderstanding at a time.

Our family therapist, Dr. Anya Sharma, a woman whose serene demeanor belied a steely resolve (and a truly impressive collection of Himalayan singing bowls), arrived with a hopeful smile and a briefcase full of what I can only describe as suspiciously shiny pamphlets. She'd been recommended by Sarah's incredibly well-connected mother, a woman who seemed to know every therapist, life coach, and spiritual advisor within a hundred-mile radius. I, however, harbored a sneaking suspicion that this particular therapist had been chosen for her ability to handle high-conflict situations, not necessarily her expertise in interracial blended families.

The session began, predictably enough, with Dr. Sharma asking us to express our feelings. Sarah, ever the optimist, started by describing her "delightful experience" attempting to make collard greens, a culinary adventure that had, in my opinion, nearly resulted in a family-wide case of food poisoning. My mother, however, took a different approach, launching into a detailed and highly critical analysis of Sarah's parenting skills, a critique that included but was not limited to Sarah's choice of bedtime stories (apparently, "Goodnight Moon" was insufficiently stimulating), her method of disciplining the children (too lenient, according to my mother), and her seemingly inexplicable fondness for lavender-scented everything.

Sarah's parents, meanwhile, remained mostly silent, their faces displaying a mixture of polite bewilderment and open horror. They were clearly grappling with the sheer audacity of my mother's directness, a quality that seemed to shock even the most seasoned therapists. Their attempts at interjecting polite counterpoints were drowned out by my mother's pronouncements, which flowed as smoothly and relentlessly as a Mississippi River flood. Dr. Sharma, bless her soul, tried valiantly to steer the conversation towards more constructive channels, but it was like trying to herd cats wearing roller skates.

Then there was the matter of my Uncle Earl, who, true to form, had somehow managed to sneak a bottle of something suspiciously brown into the therapy session, claiming it was "herbal tea" but raising my eyebrows considerably with the furtive glances he kept casting in its direction. Aunt Mildred, meanwhile, was engrossed in a heated debate with a particularly flamboyant cushion, a conversation that, while puzzling, was undeniably captivating.

The conversation took several unexpected detours. There was a lengthy discussion about the merits of different types of gravy (my mother, unsurprisingly, favored a thick, rich gravy made from scratch; Sarah's mother preferred a thin, more refined version), a sudden and impassioned argument over the proper way to fold a fitted sheet (a topic that somehow became a metaphor for our conflicting approaches to life), and a bizarre anecdote from Sarah's father about a rogue squirrel that had once stolen his dentures. By the time Dr. Sharma suggested a brief intermission, the room resembled a battlefield littered with half-eaten cookies, crumpled tissues, and a significant amount of emotional debris.

The intermission didn't exactly provide a respite. My mother and Sarah's mother engaged in a whispered conversation, their voices low but their expressions distinctly hostile. I overheard snippets of words like "inadequate," "unsuitable," and "lavender," all uttered with the kind of venom usually reserved for political opponents. Meanwhile, Uncle Earl was attempting to engage Dr. Sharma in a game of charades, using the herbal tea bottle as a prop, a gesture that, I confess, seemed less therapeutic and more like a desperate attempt at comedic relief.

The second half of the session was, if anything, even more chaotic. We somehow managed to delve into a discussion about the psychological implications of different types of cheese, a topic that somehow involved a detailed explanation of the cultural significance of cheddar in England and the surprising popularity of brie in France. My contributions to this conversation were limited to agreeing that cheese, regardless of its origin, was delicious. Dr. Sharma, clearly exasperated, attempted to gently redirect the discussion, only to be sidetracked by my Uncle Earl's sudden announcement that he was fluent in Klingon, a claim that was met with skepticism from everyone except Aunt Mildred, who seemed genuinely impressed.

Towards the end of the session, however, something unexpected happened. Amidst the chaos, amidst the flying accusations and the rogue herbal tea, there was a moment of genuine connection. Sarah confessed to feeling overwhelmed by the cultural differences and the pressure to fit into my family's unconventional dynamic. I admitted that I, too, felt the strain of navigating two vastly different family cultures. My mother, surprisingly, offered a rare moment of empathy, admitting that she had been too focused on ensuring Sarah embraced the cultural heritage she had been raised with. Sarah's parents finally broke their silence, admitting their own anxieties regarding adapting to a new culture and family dynamic.

It was a messy, chaotic, and frankly hilarious revelation, but it was a revelation nonetheless. It was in this mess of clashing personalities and cultural misunderstandings that a glimmer of understanding, of empathy, of shared humanity emerged. The session didn't miraculously solve all our problems – in fact, it probably created a few new ones – but it did reveal a common ground of shared vulnerability, shared anxieties, and shared laughter.

Dr. Sharma, upon seeing this unexpected connection, visibly relaxed. She gathered her pamphlets, her singing bowls, and her composure, and gave us one final piece of advice. "Embrace the chaos," she said, with a weary but knowing smile. "It's in the chaos that you'll often find the most profound connections." She then added, with a wink, "And maybe try the lavender tea. It's surprisingly good."

The journey towards bridging the gap between our families was far from over. It was a messy, hilarious, and at times completely baffling journey, fraught with misunderstandings, cultural clashes, and more than a few questionable culinary experiments. But within the chaos, within the laughter and the tears, lay the promise of a truly unique and, dare I say, loving family. A family held together not by perfectly aligned cultures, but by a shared understanding of the absurd, a willingness to laugh at our mistakes, and a persistent – albeit sometimes chaotic – pursuit of connection.

The therapy session, while providing a fleeting moment of shared vulnerability, did little to quell the simmering tensions within our wider community. Our unconventional relationship, a vibrant tapestry woven from two distinct cultural threads, was far from universally celebrated. In fact, it seemed to act as a lightning rod, attracting a storm of whispers, stares, and outright hostility.

The first wave of this backlash came in the form of anonymous notes slipped under our door. These weren't your typical, passive-aggressive "keep your dog quiet" missives. Oh no. These were masterpieces of thinly veiled racism, dripping with thinly-veiled bigotry, penned with the kind of vitriol usually reserved for political opponents or particularly aggressive squirrels. One note, penned in a shaky hand, simply stated, "Get out." Another was more elaborate, a rambling diatribe about the sanctity of tradition and the inherent dangers of interracial marriage, complete with underlined words and exclamation points seemingly bursting off the page. We initially tried to ignore them, burying them under a pile of junk mail and the increasingly alarming number of flyers advertising suspiciously cheap carpet cleaning services. But the notes kept coming, a relentless tide of hate mail, turning our home into what felt like a post-apocalyptic version of a Hallmark card store.

Then came the glares. The silent treatment. The pointed whispers that followed us like a persistent shadow. At the grocery store, the cashier seemed to deliberately slow down, their every move imbued with a passive-aggressive deliberateness. At church, the usual Sunday greetings were replaced with awkward silences and sidelong glances, as if we were some sort of exotic zoo exhibit. Even the friendly, neighborhood gossip, Miss Agatha Plumtree, normally a font of pleasantries and neighborhood news, now seemed to avoid us, replacing her usual cheery wave with a curt nod and a hasty retreat. It was as if our relationship had become a topic of scandalous local gossip, making us the subjects of a community-wide, involuntary reality show.

The children, bless their naive hearts, initially failed to grasp the full weight of the prejudice. They'd come home from school, recounting the curious looks, the hushed conversations they overheard, and the occasional crude drawing of stick figures that vaguely resembled us, as if their innocent understanding could somehow insulate us from the harsh realities of societal bias. But even their innocent perspectives began to shift, their carefree demeanor replaced by a cautious uncertainty, a growing awareness that their family was different, and that difference was not always celebrated.

Sarah's parents, hailing from a predominantly white, upper-middle-class suburb, were completely unprepared for the intensity of the reaction. They were accustomed to a world where differences were politely acknowledged, disagreements were resolved with calm, reasoned discourse, and a disagreement on the proper way to fold a fitted sheet didn't lead to public shaming. Their initial reaction was one of stunned disbelief, quickly followed by a growing sense of unease and, I'll admit, a certain amount of panic. They started looking at houses in a more... homogeneous neighborhood, while quietly expressing their concerns.

My own family, while far from immune to prejudice, had a much more hardened response. They were used to it, sadly. Their strategy mostly involved a combination of defiant indifference and a healthy dose of sarcastic wit. My mother, for example, took to responding to the anonymous notes with equally anonymous notes of her own, each one more hilariously sarcastic than the last. One note, in particular, was a masterpiece of passive-aggressive brilliance, describing in great detail the superior quality of her homemade collard greens, while subtly suggesting the note-writer might benefit from some nutritional counseling. Uncle Earl, on the other hand, took a more direct, and somewhat alarming approach. He started patrolling the neighborhood at night, armed with nothing but a flashlight and a suspiciously large jar of homemade pepper spray, claiming he was "deterring potential troublemakers." His efforts, though well-intentioned, were mostly unsuccessful and did little but create more anxious conversations among our neighbors.

The tension culminated during the annual town picnic, a community event normally filled with boisterous laughter, friendly competition, and an overwhelming abundance of questionable potato salad. This year, however, the atmosphere was thick with an uncomfortable silence, broken only by the occasional strained chuckle and the unnerving quiet around our picnic blanket. The stares were more intense, the whispers louder, and the distance people kept felt palpable. It was like we were attending a funeral for our own social standing. Children, who had previously been happy to share their toys and snacks, now moved away, their parents subtly guiding them away from our little corner of the park.

Even the typically jovial hotdog vendor, a man whose good humor and questionable hygiene had made him a local legend, seemed to dampen his usual charm around us. His customary greeting, a boisterous "Welcome, welcome! Get your dogs here!", was replaced by a quiet, almost apologetic "Hot dogs... anyone?" as he looked down at his feet, as if hoping we'd simply disappear.

The blatant prejudice eventually impacted even our children, who began questioning our relationship. The awkward silences, pointed glances, and seemingly random avoidance by their peers had taken a toll. They started asking questions. Why were they different? Why were people treating them differently? Why couldn't their parents be like everyone else's? These weren't easy questions to answer. These were questions that cut to the core of our relationship and forced us to confront the reality of racial prejudice in our own community.

It was at that very moment, sitting on our isolated picnic blanket, surrounded by a silent crowd, a stark contrast to the joyful atmosphere of previous years, that Sarah and I truly realized the magnitude of the task ahead of us. Bridging the gap between our families was one thing, but bridging the gap between ourselves and the wider community, a gap built on generations of ingrained prejudice and societal biases, felt like an insurmountable challenge. The journey towards acceptance, we now realized, wouldn't just be a personal one. It was going to be a battle, fought on the front lines of our own small town. And for the first time since our relationship started, we felt a true sense of fear. A fear not for our relationship, but for the well-being of our children, for their right to feel accepted in their own community. A fear born not of love, but of the harsh reality of prejudice. This challenge, however daunting, wasn't just about us; it was about the future, about fighting against the systemic biases that still clung to our community. And we knew, with a shared look of determination, that we would fight for that future. We had each other, our children, and a shared belief in the power of love and acceptance. The fight, we realized, had just begun.

The fight, as it turned out, wasn't fought on the grand stage of public protest or political rallies. It was fought in the quiet corners of our kitchen, amidst the clatter of dishes and the aroma of burnt coffee. It was fought in the hushed tones of late-night conversations, where anxieties and fears were shared, not as accusations, but as vulnerable admissions. It was a battle waged not with weapons, but with words, with compromises, and with a stubborn refusal to let prejudice win.

The first casualty of this quiet war was the concept of "my way or the highway." Sarah, raised in a household where polite disagreement was the norm, found herself struggling to navigate my family's more… robust communication style. My mother, for instance, firmly believed that the only acceptable way to cook collard greens involved a secret ingredient that remained stubbornly shrouded in mystery (and a healthy dose of sass). Sarah, accustomed to a more delicate approach to culinary arts, found herself bewildered, initially attempting to introduce her own, more refined methods. This led to a kitchen showdown of epic proportions, a culinary clash of titans that ended with a half-eaten pot of collard greens, a slightly singed cookbook, and a newfound appreciation for compromise. We eventually agreed to a rotating schedule: Sarah's refined collard greens one week, my mother's mysteriously delicious (and potentially hazardous) version the next. The result? A surprisingly delicious culinary fusion, and a significant reduction in kitchen-related warfare.

Uncle Earl, however, proved to be a more formidable opponent. His nightly neighborhood patrols, while initially intended to instill fear in the hearts of potential bigots, mostly served to alarm the local cat population. After one particularly memorable encounter with a particularly grumpy tabby, resulting in a mild pepper spray incident and a very indignant meow echoing through the night, Sarah intervened. She reasoned with him, not by dismissing his concerns, but by acknowledging them, suggesting alternative ways to address them. Instead of patrolling, they started organizing community events—barbecues, potlucks—where people could interact in a positive environment, fostering understanding and breaking down barriers. His initial resistance melted away when faced with the prospect of organizing the annual chili cook-off, a position he'd coveted for years. His patrolling ceased; his chili-making intensified.

Compromise wasn't just about appeasing opposing viewpoints; it was about finding common ground, even in the smallest of details. Sarah learned to appreciate the nuances of my family's traditions, while I embraced aspects of her upbringing. We found ourselves blending our two cultures, creating a unique family dynamic, far more interesting and enriching than either of us had imagined. We started incorporating aspects of both our cultures into our celebrations – Christmas carols intermingled with gospel hymns, Thanksgiving feasts featuring both turkey and collard greens. Even the children, initially caught in the crossfire, began to appreciate the richness of both our worlds.

Our children, initially silent observers, began to adapt, bridging the gap in their own way. They would bring home artwork, blending the styles and subjects that reflected their diverse background. They started organizing school projects that highlighted the unique aspects of both Black and white cultures, their efforts becoming a quiet, powerful act of reconciliation. It was a testament to their resilience, their ability to not only adapt but also to create something new and beautiful from two seemingly different worlds.

Sarah's parents, initially hesitant and apprehensive, began to see the depth of our commitment and the resilience of our love. They witnessed firsthand the strength of our bond, the ability to overcome challenges, and the unwavering support we gave each other. They started to actively participate in our efforts toward reconciliation. They started attending community events, gradually interacting with my family, showcasing their willingness to learn and understand. Their apprehension turned into curiosity, and curiosity into a desire to connect with a culture different from their own. Their support was not simply a matter of tolerating our relationship; it evolved into a genuine desire to embrace the cultural richness that it represented.

The turning point came during a particularly tense family gathering. It started as it often did—with a simmering tension that could be felt in the air, a silent struggle between two vastly different cultures attempting to co-exist. The conversations were stilted, filled with cautious comments and guarded smiles. Then, my mother, with a mischievous glint in her eyes, started a lively discussion about the merits of various soul food recipes, engaging Sarah's mother in a friendly culinary debate. To everyone's surprise, Sarah's mother not only participated but revealed a hidden talent for baking sweet potato pies. What followed was an unexpected culinary exchange, a sharing of recipes and stories, the air slowly clearing as the laughter and aroma of sweet potato pies filled the room. The walls between two disparate worlds began to crumble.

This wasn't a sudden transformation, a magical cure for centuries of prejudice. It was a slow, gradual process of understanding, of compromise, of shared experiences, and of a deep, abiding love that refused to be defined by societal boundaries. We continued to face prejudice, subtle slights, and occasional outbursts. But now, we faced them together, as a unit, armed with a resilience built not on ignoring the challenges, but on actively engaging with them, forging common ground and building bridges, one conversation, one compromise, one burnt collard green at a time.

The journey wasn't easy. There were still moments of frustration, misunderstandings, and disagreements. But the key was not to avoid conflict but to navigate it, to learn from it, and to emerge stronger, our bond even more resilient. We learned to celebrate our differences, to embrace our unique perspectives, and to use them to enrich, not divide. We learned that true unity wasn't about uniformity; it was about celebrating the vibrant tapestry woven from a multitude of threads.

The anonymous notes eventually stopped. The whispers faded into the background noise of everyday life. The community, though not suddenly transformed, became more accepting, more understanding. It wasn't a complete erasure of prejudice, but a softening of attitudes, a slow acceptance that grew organically from our efforts. Our children, no longer the subjects of curious stares, were embraced by their community, their differences celebrated as much as their similarities.

The annual town picnic, once a scene of silent judgment, became a vibrant celebration. Our picnic blanket was no longer an isolated island; it was a central gathering point. Our children, surrounded by friends, shared laughter and snacks, their smiles radiating a joy that reflected the success of our hard-won victory. It was a testament to the power of perseverance, of love's resilience, and the remarkable ability of a family to not just survive, but to thrive, amidst the storms of prejudice and misunderstanding. It was a testament to the power of compromise, a hard-won victory celebrated not with fanfare, but with the simple joy of a shared meal, a shared laugh, and a shared future. A future built on love, understanding, and a whole lot of delicious collard greens. And for that, we were eternally grateful. The battle was far from over, but we had found our footing, our resilience, our love acting as a powerful force that even the most ingrained prejudices could not extinguish.

The rhythm of our lives settled into a comfortable, if slightly chaotic, groove. The initial storms of disapproval had subsided, replaced by a tentative but growing acceptance. It wasn't a complete eradication of prejudice – the occasional sideways glance, the hushed whispers – but it was a significant shift, a palpable change in the atmosphere. And at the heart of this shift was the simple joy of shared experiences.

We discovered a mutual love for old movies, spending countless nights curled up on the couch, lost in the world of black and white classics and cheesy romantic comedies. Sarah, a connoisseur of classic Hollywood, introduced me to the world of Katharine Hepburn and Cary Grant, while I, in return, shared the soulful rhythms of classic soul music and the vibrant energy of 1970s blaxploitation films. These shared moments, these quiet evenings, became our sanctuary, a space where the anxieties and stresses of the outside world melted away, replaced by laughter and shared appreciation. It was in these moments, amongst the flickering images on the screen and the comforting silence between us, that we truly connected.

Our weekends became a tapestry of shared adventures. We'd pack up the car, the kids bouncing in the backseat, and head off on spontaneous road trips, exploring hidden gems and discovering new corners of our state. We'd visit antique shops, Sarah's passion for vintage treasures igniting my own curiosity. We'd attend local farmers' markets, her appreciation for fresh, organic produce colliding with my love of trying new spices and street food. These shared activities weren't just about doing things together; they were about learning from each other, about expanding our horizons, and about creating memories that would forever bind us.

Evenings were a testament to our unique blend of cultures. We'd alternate between Sarah's sophisticated dinner parties, where candlelight and fine wine set the mood, and my more boisterous family gatherings, filled with soul food, laughter, and spontaneous bursts of gospel singing. The children thrived in this blend, effortlessly switching between formal settings and lively family reunions. They developed a remarkable adaptability, a cultural fluency that was both inspiring and heartwarming.

One Saturday morning, inspired by a vintage cookbook Sarah had discovered, we embarked on a joint baking project. The kitchen transformed into a whirlwind of flour, sugar, and a healthy dose of sibling rivalry. The objective: a magnificent multi-layered cake that would be a fusion of Sarah's refined baking skills and my mother's secret ingredient collard green cake recipe. (Yes, you read that right. My mother had a collard green cake recipe. It was...an experience.) The result was less than perfect, aesthetically speaking, but the laughter that erupted from the kitchen was the best icing. It was a messy, chaotic display of creativity, a perfect reflection of our blended family.

Beyond the shared activities, we found common ground in our shared values. Our commitment to family, our belief in education, and our passion for social justice became the pillars that supported our relationship. We'd often discuss current events, engaging in lively debates that were always respectful, even when passionate. These conversations helped us to understand each other's perspectives, to appreciate the nuances of our differing viewpoints, and to grow together intellectually and emotionally.

We also realized that finding common ground wasn't always about grand gestures or sweeping declarations. It was often found in the smallest moments, the quiet gestures of love and support. A shared cup of coffee in the morning, a whispered word of encouragement before a challenging day, a tender touch during a moment of sadness. These were the threads that wove our lives together, creating a bond that was unbreakable, a love that was undeniable.

This wasn't to say that challenges disappeared. There were still moments of friction, of misunderstandings, of clashing cultures. But our ability to navigate these challenges had transformed. We were no longer reactive, responding defensively to differences. Instead, we had learned to approach disagreements with empathy and understanding, recognizing that differences weren't necessarily obstacles but opportunities for growth and connection.

Sarah's parents, having witnessed our resilience and our commitment to each other, had become ardent supporters. They were no longer just tolerating our relationship; they were actively embracing it, participating in our family gatherings, sharing meals, and even attempting to master the art of collard greens (with varying degrees of success). Their initial reservations had melted away, replaced by a genuine affection for our family and a newfound appreciation for the richness of our blended culture.

Our children, once caught in the crossfire of cultural clashes, flourished. They became bridges, effortlessly navigating the world of two cultures, blending traditions, and creating a unique identity that reflected their diverse heritage. They were a testament to the power of love, resilience, and adaptation.

One particularly memorable evening, as we sat around the dinner table, sharing stories and laughter, my daughter proudly presented a school project—a vibrant collage that showcased the history of both Black and white music, blending blues with classical, gospel with folk. It was a beautiful representation of the unique tapestry of our family, a reflection of the beauty that emerges when two different worlds converge. It was a moment of profound pride, a testament to the progress we had made, a symbol of the common ground we had painstakingly built.

The journey hadn't been easy, but it had been incredibly rewarding. We had faced prejudice, misunderstandings, and societal expectations with grace and resilience. We had found common ground not by eliminating our differences, but by celebrating them, by embracing the unique perspectives that enriched our lives. Our family wasn't just a blend of two cultures; it was a vibrant testament to the power of love, understanding, and the unwavering commitment to build bridges, one conversation, one compromise, one delicious (and sometimes slightly burnt) collard green cake at a time. The journey was ongoing, but the destination – a family bound by love and understanding – was within reach, shimmering with the promise of a future filled with laughter, joy, and the enduring warmth of a truly blended family. And in the heart of it all, was the simple, profound truth that love, in its truest form, conquers all.

The quiet evenings, the shared laughter, the collaborative kitchen disasters—these were the moments that defined us, the building blocks of a love story that defied expectations and blossomed into something truly extraordinary. It was a testament not only to our love but to the power of finding common ground, of embracing differences, and of creating a family that celebrated the vibrant tapestry of its diverse heritage. And that, in itself, was a story worth telling, a story worth living, a story that continued to unfold, one day, one shared experience, one delicious collard green cake at a time.

Chapter 4: Love in the Time of Stereotypes

The seemingly idyllic peace of our blended family life wasn't without its cracks. The subtle slights, the whispered comments, the occasional outright hostility – these were the persistent undercurrents that threatened to disrupt the calm. We'd reached a point where polite tolerance wasn't enough; it was time to address the elephant in the room, or rather, the elephants – a whole herd of them, trumpeting their prejudices with varying degrees of subtlety.

It started with Aunt Mildred. Aunt Mildred, Sarah's maternal aunt, was a woman of staunch opinions and even stancher disapproval of our union. Her disapproval wasn't subtle. It was a force of nature, a hurricane of disapproval wrapped in a floral print dress and smelling faintly of lavender and disdain. One particularly fraught family gathering, Aunt Mildred, fueled by several glasses of sherry and a lifetime of ingrained biases, decided to launch a full-scale assault on our relationship, disguised as a casual inquiry.

"So, Marcus," she began, her voice dripping with a saccharine sweetness that only amplified the venom within, "how are you... *adjusting* to... well, you know... *everything*?" The "everything" hung heavy in the air, a pregnant pause filled with unspoken judgments and veiled accusations.

I decided to meet her head-on, armed with nothing but a wry smile and a healthy dose of wit. "Adjusting marvelously, Aunt Mildred," I replied, my tone as smooth and even as possible, "although I must admit, I'm still trying to decipher the intricacies of your sherry-fueled pronouncements. Is it a new form of interpretive dance, or a veiled attempt at passive-aggressive communication? Perhaps a doctoral thesis awaits!"

The room erupted in a mixture of gasps and stifled laughter. Even Sarah, who knew my penchant for a perfectly timed jab, looked slightly surprised. Aunt Mildred, momentarily speechless, sputtered, her carefully crafted facade of polite concern crumbling into a heap of indignant fury. The ensuing conversation, while not exactly amicable, was certainly memorable. It was a lesson in how to confront prejudice with humor, to use wit as a weapon against ignorance.

The battle with Aunt Mildred, however, was just the beginning. There were other skirmishes to be fought, other prejudices to be challenged. The grocery store checkout line became an unexpected battleground. A surly cashier, clearly flustered by the sight of a black man and a white woman shopping together, fumbled with the bags, muttering something under her breath about "mixed families" and "the way things should be." I chose a different approach this time, not a witty retort, but a quiet, steady voice.

"Excuse me," I said, my tone calm but firm, "did you just say something about 'the way things should be'? Because I'd like to suggest that the way things *should* be is everyone treated with respect, regardless of their race or who they choose to love. Is there something I can help you with, or are you perhaps having a difficult day?"

The cashier, caught off guard by my directness, mumbled an apology and finished the transaction with a noticeably more respectful demeanor. It was a small victory, but it was significant. It proved that sometimes, the most effective way to confront prejudice is with quiet, unwavering assertiveness.

These encounters were far from isolated incidents. We encountered subtle forms of prejudice everywhere: the hesitant smiles, the lingering stares, the whispered comments that followed us like shadows. Each one was a tiny sting, a constant reminder of the societal biases that still permeated our world.

One particularly disheartening encounter occurred at a family reunion on Sarah's side. While most of her family had warmed to me, some distant relatives harbored an unspoken animosity. One of Sarah's cousins, a man named Richard, a man who seemed to take great pride in his self-proclaimed traditional values, made a point of excluding me from conversations, ignoring my attempts at polite interaction. His wife, equally dismissive, treated me like a piece of furniture, a fixture in the room but devoid of any real presence.

That day, I realized that humor wasn't always the answer. Sometimes, direct confrontation was necessary. After a particularly pointed exclusion from a family discussion about upcoming renovations to their summer home, I had enough. I simply walked over to Richard and his wife, stared them both down, and said with a level voice, "Your quiet contempt is as obvious as your uncomfortable silence. If you have something to say to me, say it. If not, kindly spare yourselves and me the passive-aggressive charade."

The silence that followed was deafening. Their faces were a mixture of shock and defensiveness, their previous air of smug superiority dissolving into an uncomfortable awareness of their own bigotry. The encounter wasn't pleasant but it set a boundary. From that moment on, while not friendly, their behavior toward me significantly changed. The blatant exclusion stopped.

These confrontations weren't always easy, often leaving me emotionally drained, but they were necessary. They were a testament to our resolve, our commitment to not allowing prejudice to dictate our lives or damage our love. We learned to fight back, to stand up for ourselves and for our relationship, using a combination of humor, assertiveness, and unwavering love.

The journey wasn't always smooth, but the shared laughter, the inside jokes forged in the heat of these battles, became our own private victories. These small victories, accumulated over time, built a powerful bulwark against the tide of prejudice. They became a testament to the power of love and resilience, to the enduring strength of a relationship that dared to defy expectations. And the collard green cake, well, it continued to be a source of both culinary adventures and family bonding, a quirky symbol of our unlikely, and undeniably hilarious, family unit. The cake, it seemed, was a metaphor for our journey: sometimes messy, sometimes burnt, but always uniquely delicious in its own way.

But the tide began to turn, surprisingly, not from within our immediate families, but from the most unexpected of quarters. It started with Mr. Henderson, the gruff, seemingly unapproachable owner of the local hardware store. Mr. Henderson, a man whose taciturn nature was only surpassed by his impressive collection of rusty tools, was a fixture in our neighborhood. He'd seen it all, weathered every storm, and seemed impervious to anything that didn't involve plumbing or fixing leaky faucets. I figured he was the last person who'd offer us any sort of support.

One particularly rainy Tuesday, Sarah and I were at his store, searching for a replacement part for our perpetually malfunctioning washing machine. The usual awkward silence hung heavy between us as he measured bolts and rattled off prices. As I fumbled with my wallet, a small, almost imperceptible tremor ran through his usually stoic demeanor. He cleared his throat, his gaze drifting to a faded photograph tucked into the corner of his cash register. It was a picture of him, younger, with a woman who bore a striking resemblance to Sarah – fair-skinned, with bright, intelligent eyes.

"That's my… late wife," he said, the words barely a whisper. He paused, a rare crack in his normally impenetrable armor. "She… she was from England. Met her during the war. People… people weren't always understanding." He gave a rueful shrug, his eyes distant. "Never thought I'd see the day… a fella like you… with a woman like your wife. But you know… love finds a way, doesn't it? It always does."

His simple statement, devoid of any grand pronouncements or platitudes, held more weight than any sermon I'd ever heard. It was a quiet acknowledgment, a simple understanding born from a shared experience of navigating a world that didn't always make sense. The unspoken empathy in his words was profoundly moving. It was a validation that transcended race, transcending prejudice, a quiet affirmation that our love, despite the odds, was valid.

From then on, Mr. Henderson became an unlikely ally. He wasn't effusive, he never offered unsolicited advice, but his subtle acts of kindness spoke volumes. He'd always give us the best deals on our hardware purchases, offer a knowing nod when he saw us in town, a silent affirmation of our journey. He was our silent guardian, our quiet champion, a man who, through his own experiences, understood the power and resilience of love in the face of adversity.

Unexpected alliances continued to blossom in the most surprising places. Mrs. Rodriguez, our next-door neighbor, a vibrant woman known for her fiery temperament and even fierier tamales, became an unexpected confidante. Initially, her curiosity about our interracial marriage bordered on nosiness. But her questions, though initially probing, were never malicious. As we shared our experiences, our struggles, our triumphs, she became a surprising source of strength and unwavering support. She'd share stories from her own family's immigration experiences, stories of prejudice and perseverance, of finding solace in community.

"Love don't care about the color of your skin, mija," she'd say, her voice filled with a wisdom born from years of life experiences. "It's about the heart, the soul. The rest is just noise." Her tamales became a regular offering, a symbol of her acceptance, her quiet way of saying, "You belong here."

Then there was the unlikely friendship with young Elijah, a bright-eyed, energetic boy who lived across the street. Elijah's family was deeply rooted in the community, steeped in traditions and a conservative worldview. Initially, they were hesitant about our presence in the neighborhood, casting apprehensive glances whenever we were outside. But Elijah, undeterred by adult prejudices, was drawn to Sarah's infectious laughter and my silly attempts at playing catch with him.

He became our unofficial ambassador of goodwill, a small but potent force against the prevailing biases. He'd invite me to play basketball with his friends, seamlessly integrating me into their games, effortlessly erasing the lines of difference. He'd often bring Sarah flowers he'd picked from his mother's garden, small gestures of kindness that chipped away at the barriers between our families. Elijah became a testament to the power of children's unfiltered innocence, a pure reflection of the world as it should be – devoid of prejudice, brimming with empathy.

These unlikely friendships became our solace, our anchors in a world that wasn't always kind. They proved that acceptance, true acceptance, wasn't confined to those who shared our background, our history, or our beliefs. It came from unexpected places, from people who had navigated their own struggles and understood the profound strength in defying expectations.

It became apparent that the fight against prejudice wasn't a solitary endeavor; it was a collective effort. The quiet support of Mr. Henderson, the unwavering friendship of Mrs. Rodriguez, and Elijah's unassuming kindness created a network of unexpected allies, people who, through their actions and words, silently championed our love, our family. They showed that even in the face of adversity, empathy, understanding, and ultimately, love, could bloom in the most unexpected of places.

The journey wasn't without its bumps; there were still moments of discomfort, of subtle slights that cut deep. But armed with our love, our humor, and our growing circle of unexpected allies, we began to feel stronger, more resilient. We learned that fighting prejudice wasn't about winning every battle; it was about showing up, about choosing love over hate, about creating space for acceptance, even in the smallest of ways.

One evening, as Sarah and I sat on our porch, watching Elijah and his friends play basketball under the warm glow of the setting sun, I realized the profound impact of these unexpected friendships. It wasn't just about overcoming prejudice; it was about the unexpected ways in which love and acceptance could blossom, enriching our lives beyond our wildest expectations.

It was in those moments, surrounded by the sound of children's laughter and the comforting presence of our unexpected allies, that I truly understood the power of community, the strength that comes from forging connections beyond perceived boundaries. It was a testament to the enduring power of love and the remarkable ability of the human spirit to overcome prejudice, one unexpected friendship at a time. The fight wasn't over, but with each unexpected ally, with each small act of kindness, we felt a little stronger, a little more hopeful, a little more certain that love, in all its messy, unpredictable glory, would ultimately prevail. And perhaps, just perhaps, we could even share some of that love, that understanding, and that resilience with others along the way.

The collard green cake, once a symbol of our differences, became a unifying force. We started making extra batches, sharing them with Mr. Henderson, Mrs. Rodriguez, and even some of the more hesitant members of Sarah's family. The sweet aroma of the cake, the warmth of sharing it with others, became another small but meaningful step in our journey towards fostering acceptance and understanding. It was a symbol of our shared experiences, a reminder that even the most unexpected alliances could lead to delicious and heartwarming results.

The unexpected alliances continued to grow, weaving a vibrant tapestry of acceptance around our unconventional family. It wasn't just about our immediate circle; the ripple effect of our interracial marriage began to touch lives far beyond our own. The change wasn't dramatic, not a sudden societal shift, but a quiet revolution, a slow but steady erosion of prejudice, one kind word, one shared smile, one collard green cake at a time.

It began with small gestures. The local librarian, a quiet woman with a penchant for historical fiction, started featuring more diverse books in the children's section. She'd even organized a small book reading event featuring authors from diverse backgrounds, an initiative she admitted she'd never considered before meeting Sarah and me. Her explanation was simple: "Seeing your family... it made me realize how limited our selection was, how important it was to show kids different perspectives, different stories." This wasn't some grand public declaration; it was a personal awakening, a subtle shift in perspective fueled by our very existence.

Then came the community potluck. Initially, the atmosphere was stiff, the usual polite but distant interactions of a community trying to navigate the unfamiliar. But Sarah, with her infectious laughter and her talent for making even the most skeptical individuals feel welcome, broke the ice. She brought a giant platter of her famous sweet potato pie, a culinary bridge that transcended cultural differences. The pie, along with our own collard green cake (now a staple of our community gatherings), sparked conversations, leading to shared stories, shared laughter, and a shared sense of community. The potluck, once a potential minefield of awkward silences and strained smiles, became a celebration of diversity, a testament to the power of shared food and shared experiences.

Our impact even reached the local school. Sarah, a gifted artist, volunteered to teach an art class, introducing the children to a broader range of artistic styles and perspectives. She showcased the work of Black artists, of women artists, of artists from different cultures, expanding the children's artistic horizons and, in doing so, their worldviews. The subtle integration of diversity into the curriculum was a testament to the power of quiet influence, of showing, rather than telling, the beauty and richness of a multicultural society.

The local newspaper, initially hesitant to feature our story, finally published an article about our family. It wasn't a sensationalist exposé, but a simple human interest piece, highlighting the joy, the challenges, and the resilience of our unconventional family. The article, surprisingly, generated a wave of positive feedback, letters pouring in from readers sharing their own experiences with prejudice, their own struggles, and their own victories in overcoming societal biases. Our story, it turned out, resonated with many, reminding them that love knows no boundaries and that breaking down barriers requires courage, persistence, and a whole lot of laughter.

One evening, while attending a community theater production, we noticed a subtle shift in the audience demographic. More people of color were attending, more families with interracial couples were present. The theater, once a predominantly white space, was slowly but surely becoming a more inclusive venue, a reflection of the changing social landscape of our community. The theater's director later confessed that our presence, our quiet acceptance, had inspired them to actively seek out more diverse plays and to reach out to broader communities, ensuring a more representative portrayal of the local population.

It wasn't just about big, sweeping changes. It was about the small, incremental shifts – a kind word from a neighbor, a shared smile from a stranger, a helping hand from an unexpected ally. These seemingly insignificant gestures created a wave of acceptance, a domino effect of positive change that spread slowly but surely through our community.

Sarah's family, once deeply skeptical and resistant to our relationship, gradually began to understand and accept. The initial skepticism didn't vanish overnight, but the frequent visits, the shared meals, and the shared laughter gradually chipped away at their prejudices. They started seeing Sarah not just as a wife, but as a mother, a daughter-in-law, and a member of their extended family. The shared experiences, the shared joy of raising our children, forged a bond stronger than any initial resistance. The collard green cake, once a symbol of our differences, now represented their own evolving understanding and acceptance.

Our journey wasn't simply about overcoming our own personal challenges; it was about inspiring others to challenge their own biases and preconceived notions. It was about demonstrating that love, true love, transcends cultural differences and societal expectations. It was about showing that a family, any family, can be built on mutual respect, understanding, and a healthy dose of humor. We became, almost unwittingly, symbols of hope and change, inspiring others to embrace diversity and celebrate the richness of human experience.

The laughter at our family gatherings, once laced with tension and awkwardness, was now filled with genuine joy and shared experiences. The children, blissfully unaware of the initial prejudice, embraced our blended family with an innocence that served as a constant reminder of the world as it should be – a world without boundaries, a world filled with love, acceptance, and laughter.

Our journey to break down barriers wasn't a sprint; it was a marathon. There were still moments of prejudice, of subtle slights, of lingering biases. But with each act of kindness, each unexpected alliance, each shared meal, we grew stronger, more resilient. We learned that the fight against prejudice wasn't just about winning battles; it was about showing up, about choosing empathy over judgment, about fostering understanding, one heart at a time.

Our story wasn't just about a Black man and a white woman falling in love; it was a testament to the power of love to overcome societal barriers, a celebration of the unexpected allies who helped us along the way, and a reminder that even the smallest acts of kindness can have a profound and lasting impact. The collard green cake, now a symbol of our resilience and our shared journey, continued to be a delicious metaphor for the sweet taste of victory, a victory not just for us, but for the entire community that learned to embrace the diversity that ultimately enriched all of our lives. Our story, in its messy, unpredictable, and utterly hilarious glory, was a reminder that love, laughter, and a whole lot of collard green cake can conquer even the most deeply ingrained stereotypes. And that, my friends, is a story worth telling, a story worth celebrating, and a story that deserves a sequel. Or maybe a sitcom.

The kids, bless their innocent hearts, were the ultimate ambassadors of our blended family. They didn't see color, or rather, they saw color as just... color. A rainbow of possibilities, not a barrier. Their friends reflected this beautiful blend – a kaleidoscope of cultures and backgrounds that enriched their lives and ours. We had playdates where we'd hear Swahili lullabies mingling with Irish folk songs, where Italian pasta sat alongside Jamaican jerk chicken on the table, a delicious melting pot of flavors and traditions.

One particular incident stands out. It was Halloween, and the kids were insistent on dressing up as characters from their favorite books. Our oldest, Maya, was determined to be Harriet Tubman, a choice that filled me with immense pride. Liam, my stepson, went as a courageous knight from a medieval tale, his costume complete with a self-made plastic sword. The younger ones, twins, chose to be a pair of mischievous pandas.

That night, as we trick-or-treated, we encountered a few skeptical glances, the occasional mumbled comment. But the kids, oblivious to any negativity, enthusiastically shared their stories, their costumes sparking conversations instead of causing discomfort. Maya, in her Harriet Tubman costume, proudly told strangers about her bravery and her fight for freedom, inspiring smiles and awe. Liam, with his plastic sword, told tales of chivalry, prompting laughter and admiration. The twins, with their panda antics, charmed everyone into fits of giggles, bridging cultural gaps with their simple joy.

We organized a family trip to a local cultural festival. It was a vibrant explosion of colors, music, and food, showcasing the rich tapestry of our city's diverse population. The kids were enthralled, dancing to unfamiliar rhythms, sampling exotic foods, and learning about traditions from different parts of the world. Sarah and I took turns explaining the significance of different cultural practices, emphasizing the beauty and richness of each one.

Sarah, a natural teacher, excelled at explaining the cultural nuances to her side of the family, who were initially apprehensive about the festival. But witnessing the kids' delight, their unbridled joy at embracing new experiences, melted away much of the apprehension. They started engaging, asking questions, and slowly but surely, their initial reticence gave way to curiosity and appreciation.

The festival became a turning point. We weren't just showcasing cultural diversity; we were actively experiencing it, immersing ourselves in its vibrancy. It was an education, not only for the kids but for all of us. We learned about traditions we'd never encountered, tasted foods that expanded our culinary horizons, and connected with people from backgrounds vastly different from our own.

Later that year, Sarah's family hosted a Christmas gathering. A year earlier, the atmosphere had been tense, a clash of cultures and expectations. But this year, it was remarkably different. The kids, armed with their newfound knowledge of various cultural traditions, helped decorate the Christmas tree with ornaments representing their different heritages – Kwanzaa symbols alongside Christmas baubles, dreidels near Santa figurines.

They enthusiastically explained the origins and significance of each decoration, bridging the gap between traditions and fostering understanding. Sarah's mother, who had once been hesitant to embrace our blended family, was clearly moved by their initiative. She commented on how their enthusiasm had opened her eyes to the beauty of diversity. This wasn't just tolerance; it was active appreciation.

Our home became a vibrant hub of cultural exchange. We celebrated Kwanzaa with its traditional libations and storytelling, Hanukkah with its menorah and latkes, and Christmas with its carols and gifts. We didn't shy away from differences; instead, we embraced them, integrating them into our daily lives.

We introduced our children to diverse authors and musicians. The bedtime stories weren't limited to traditional fairy tales; we delved into stories representing diverse cultures and backgrounds. We listened to music from around the world, encouraging the kids to explore different genres and appreciate the universality of music. We exposed them to different artistic forms, from African masks to Japanese calligraphy, showing them the beauty and creativity of human expression across cultures.

This wasn't about erasing our own identities; it was about enriching them with the experiences of others. We encouraged the kids to take pride in their heritage, to understand their own roots while celebrating the richness of other cultures. We taught them that difference wasn't something to fear but something to celebrate, something that made the world a more vibrant and interesting place.

One evening, while discussing a particularly challenging situation with Sarah, she shared an insight that profoundly impacted me. "Marcus," she said, "it's not about conforming or pretending to be something we're not. It's about creating a space where our differences are not only tolerated but celebrated. It's about finding ways to blend our cultures, creating something new and beautiful, something unique to our family."

Her words resonated deeply. We weren't trying to erase our differences; we were using them as a canvas, creating a vibrant masterpiece of a family. We celebrated our different foods, our different music, our different traditions, each enriching the other, creating a unique and harmonious blend. This wasn't just about acceptance; it was about celebrating the beauty of our differences, turning what society might have viewed as challenges into a tapestry of vibrant colors, proving that love truly does transcend all boundaries. The journey wasn't without its bumps – misunderstandings, awkward moments, and the occasional clash of opinions still occurred. But these moments became opportunities for growth, for learning, and for deepening our understanding of each other and of ourselves.

The children, our little cultural ambassadors, became a constant source of inspiration, teaching us the importance of empathy, understanding, and the beauty of diversity. They showed us that cultural differences didn't have to be obstacles, but rather, stepping stones to a richer, more fulfilling life. They taught us, more than anything, that love transcends all boundaries, a love strengthened and enriched by celebrating the beautiful mosaic of our unique family. And as our family grew, so did our understanding, our appreciation, and our unyielding love for each other. The journey continues, a testament to the power of love, understanding, and the delicious taste of collard greens and sweet potato pie shared across cultural divides. Our story, our family, a testament to the idea that love truly conquers all, even stereotypes. And yes, even the most awkward of family gatherings can become joyous celebrations, proving that diversity, when embraced, creates not just a family, but a masterpiece.

The following Christmas, Sarah's family gathering felt less like a minefield and more like a vibrant, slightly chaotic, family reunion. Sarah's mother, bless her heart, even attempted a variation of my mother's famous collard greens recipe, a gesture that, while slightly off in terms of seasoning, spoke volumes about her growing acceptance. The kids, of course, were the stars of the show, effortlessly navigating the cultural nuances with the grace of seasoned diplomats. They explained the significance of Kwanzaa, detailing the principles of unity and self-determination, while simultaneously regaling their cousins with tales of Hanukkah's miracle and the symbolic lighting of the menorah. Liam, ever the charmer, even managed to teach his cousins a few Swahili phrases, much to the amusement of everyone present.

This wasn't merely tolerance; it was a genuine appreciation for the richness of our blended heritage. We weren't erasing our differences; we were weaving them together, creating a vibrant tapestry of traditions and experiences that enriched our lives in unexpected ways. Sarah and I, no longer burdened by the weight of societal expectations, found ourselves more comfortable in our own skins, more confident in our relationship, and more deeply in love. We had discovered the secret ingredient to our successful union: the acceptance, not just of each other, but of our diverse identities.

One evening, as we sat on the porch, sipping sweet tea and watching the fireflies dance in the twilight, Sarah confessed, "You know, Marcus, I used to worry about how our differences would affect our family. I worried about the stereotypes, the judgment, the potential conflicts. But looking at our kids, seeing how effortlessly they embrace their heritage and celebrate our differences, it's given me a new perspective." Her words were a balm to my soul, a testament to the power of love and acceptance.

We realized that embracing our differences wasn't about compromising our identities but about adding to the richness of our lives. It was about learning from each other, sharing experiences, and fostering a deep understanding and respect for our respective cultures. It was about creating a space where our children could grow up feeling proud of their heritage, confident in their identity, and secure in the love and acceptance of their family.

This newfound understanding didn't magically erase all challenges. There were still moments of awkwardness, misunderstandings, and even occasional family squabbles. But these moments, once sources of anxiety and stress, became opportunities for growth, for learning, and for strengthening our bond. We learned to communicate more effectively, to listen more attentively, and to appreciate the different perspectives that enriched our family dynamic. We learned to laugh at our own foibles and celebrate our triumphs, creating a culture of mutual respect and understanding.

The evolution of our relationship was a testament to our individual growth and the strength of our commitment. We learned to challenge stereotypes, not through anger or defensiveness, but through education and understanding. We actively sought opportunities to educate ourselves and others about the richness of our diverse backgrounds, dispelling myths and fostering appreciation.

Sarah actively participated in events celebrating Black culture, immersing herself in the music, food, and traditions. I, in turn, embraced aspects of her white, middle-class upbringing, finding common ground and understanding amidst our differences. We didn't try to erase or minimize our individual identities; instead, we celebrated them, finding ways to weave them together to create a unique and harmonious whole.

Our children became our greatest teachers. They displayed an innate ability to bridge cultural divides, fostering understanding and appreciation for different backgrounds. They became ambassadors of tolerance, their simple, unfiltered acceptance a powerful lesson for all of us. They became a testament to the idea that love, family, and belonging are not defined by race or background but by the strength of the bonds we forge.

The shift wasn't sudden or dramatic. It was a gradual evolution, a process of understanding, learning, and growth. It was a journey of self-discovery, where we learned to embrace our individual identities while strengthening our bond as a couple. It was about recognizing that our differences, instead of dividing us, created a beautiful, vibrant, and enriching mosaic.

The transition wasn't always easy. There were moments of frustration, misunderstandings, and even conflict. But instead of letting these differences drive us apart, we chose to confront them with honesty, patience, and a deep commitment to our love for each other and for our family.

We sought the support of friends and family who understood and appreciated our journey. We found comfort in shared experiences, mutual support, and the knowledge that we weren't alone. We surrounded ourselves with people who celebrated our differences, fostering a community that embraced and respected our unique family dynamic.

We started small, making conscious efforts to celebrate each other's cultural backgrounds and traditions. We learned to cook each other's favorite dishes, sharing recipes and stories. We listened to each other's music, appreciating the nuances and emotions expressed in different genres. We learned to appreciate the value of shared experiences, fostering a deeper understanding and connection.

Over time, the lines blurred, the differences became less significant, and the similarities more pronounced. We discovered a shared appreciation for family, laughter, and the simple joys of life. We found a common language in love, respect, and mutual understanding.

Our story isn't just about overcoming racial differences; it's about the transformative power of love, the importance of embracing diversity, and the strength that comes from a united family. It's about the understanding that challenges and differences, when confronted with open minds and hearts, can become opportunities for growth and deeper connection.

We learned that love isn't about erasing differences but celebrating them. It's about acknowledging and appreciating the unique contributions each individual brings to the relationship and the family. It's about understanding that true unity lies not in conformity but in the rich tapestry of diverse experiences and perspectives. It's about accepting the messy, complicated, beautiful reality of a blended family, embracing the challenges, and celebrating the victories, together.

Our home became a microcosm of the world, a haven where different cultures coexisted, creating a unique and vibrant family culture. We embraced the fusion of our backgrounds, creating new traditions that reflected our diverse heritage. Our children grew up surrounded by a rich tapestry of traditions, languages, and perspectives, learning to appreciate the beauty of difference.

The journey wasn't always smooth, but it was certainly an adventure, one that filled our lives with joy, laughter, and a profound appreciation for the diverse tapestry of human experience. And as we look back on our journey, we realize that the most valuable lesson we learned wasn't about overcoming stereotypes, but about discovering the profound beauty of embracing our identities, together. Our story is a testament to the power of love, acceptance, and the remarkable ability of a blended family to create something beautiful, unique, and undeniably their own. Our family, a testament to the strength of love, transcending boundaries and celebrating the vibrant mosaic of our shared lives. A story of overcoming stereotypes, not by ignoring them, but by celebrating the very differences that made our family so incredibly rich and special. A testament to the enduring power of love, a love that blossomed and thrived, nurtured by the acceptance and celebration of our unique identities.

Chapter 5: A New Generation

The arrival of our first grandchild, little Maya, was a joyous occasion, a tiny human embodiment of our blended family's unique tapestry. But with her arrival came a new set of challenges, a whole new level of cultural negotiation. Maya, bless her heart, was already exhibiting a remarkable fluidity between languages, seamlessly switching between Swahili and English, often throwing in a smattering of Yiddish from her great-aunt Esther's frequent visits. This linguistic dexterity was adorable, but it also highlighted the complexities of raising bicultural children in a world that often struggles to understand such fluidity.

Sarah's parents, ever the enthusiastic grandparents, were initially hesitant about some of our traditions. They were bewildered by the vibrant colours and intricate beadwork of the Kwanzaa kinara, and initially struggled with the nuances of Swahili greetings. It wasn't that they were resistant; they were simply unfamiliar. It took patience, explanation, and a healthy dose of humor to bridge the gap. We explained the symbolism behind Kwanzaa, the principles of unity, self-determination, and collective responsibility. We introduced them to the rhythms and melodies of Swahili songs, and the delicious flavors of traditional dishes. Gradually, their apprehension melted away, replaced by a genuine curiosity and appreciation for our heritage.

My mother, on the other hand, was a natural. She embraced Sarah's family with open arms, eagerly sharing her culinary expertise and passing down generations of family recipes. She'd even started incorporating some of Sarah's family's culinary traditions into her own repertoire. Imagine collard greens with a subtle hint of rosemary and thyme – a delightful fusion that surprised even me.

The kids, Liam and Chloe, were equally adept at navigating this cultural melting pot. They became the ultimate translators, explaining nuances of both cultures to their grandparents, and their cousins. They would patiently explain the symbolism behind Hanukkah's menorah, the significance of the eight nights of celebration, and then effortlessly switch to explaining the meaning of the seven principles of Kwanzaa. Their ability to seamlessly transition between cultures was a testament to their upbringing, a powerful demonstration of the strength and beauty of a blended family.

However, the path wasn't always paved with sunshine and cultural harmony. There were disagreements, moments of frustration, and even the occasional clash of traditions. One particularly memorable incident involved a disagreement over Maya's first birthday celebration. Sarah's family envisioned a traditional tea party with delicate finger sandwiches and dainty cakes, while my family envisioned a lively affair with African drumming, storytelling, and a mountain of delicious Swahili delicacies. The compromise? A dual celebration; a smaller, more traditional tea party in the afternoon, followed by a vibrant, rhythmic evening celebration that blended the best of both worlds. It was a testament to our evolving ability to negotiate and find common ground.

The challenges extended beyond just family gatherings. Navigating the complexities of societal expectations proved challenging. We found ourselves frequently explaining the intricacies of our family dynamic to teachers, friends, and even casual acquaintances. There were awkward questions, puzzled looks, and sometimes even outright prejudice. But we tackled these challenges head-on, educating those who were willing to learn, and respectfully dismissing those who were not.

We realized that raising our children in this diverse environment required proactive education and open communication. We sought out resources to help us navigate the complexities of bicultural parenting, reading books, attending workshops, and connecting with other families who shared similar experiences. We also made a conscious effort to expose our children to a broad range of cultures and perspectives. We enrolled them in schools with diverse student populations, took them on trips to museums and cultural centers, and encouraged them to interact with people from different backgrounds.

The children's schooling presented its own set of challenges and rewards. We encountered situations where Liam and Chloe's unique cultural background wasn't fully understood or appreciated by some teachers and classmates. There were misunderstandings about their language skills, their cultural traditions, and even their names. But we were proactive in advocating for our children and educating the school community about the richness and value of their bicultural heritage. We arranged meetings with teachers to explain our children's backgrounds, shared relevant resources, and even provided presentations to the class about our family's cultural traditions.

We also realized that raising bicultural children wasn't just about exposing them to different cultures; it was also about helping them develop a strong sense of self-identity. We nurtured their pride in their heritage, encouraging them to embrace their cultural backgrounds and celebrate their unique identities. We made sure they had access to books, music, and other resources that represented their diverse cultural backgrounds. We talked openly and honestly with them about race, culture, and identity, helping them develop a strong sense of self-worth and belonging.

The journey wasn't always easy, but it was incredibly rewarding. Watching our children navigate the complexities of their bicultural identities with confidence and grace was a source of immense pride. They became natural ambassadors of cultural understanding, demonstrating to others the beauty and richness of diversity. Their effortless blend of languages, traditions, and perspectives became a testament to the success of our blended family's journey.

It wasn't just about tolerance; it was about celebrating the differences that made our family unique. It was about acknowledging the complexities, the occasional clashes, and the moments of confusion, all while embracing the richness and vibrancy of our multi-faceted identity. It was a journey of constant learning, adaptation, and a deep-seated appreciation for the beauty of diversity. We created a home where differences were not just tolerated, but celebrated, fostering an environment where our children could flourish and grow into confident, well-rounded individuals who embraced their unique heritage.

We learned to embrace the unexpected detours and celebrate the serendipitous moments of understanding and connection. We realized that the strength of our family didn't lie in the absence of challenges, but in our ability to navigate them together, learning and growing from every experience. The challenges, once obstacles, became opportunities for growth, for deeper understanding, and for strengthening the bonds that held our family together. Our unique family structure became a testament to the power of love, acceptance, and the ability to create a beautiful, vibrant, and harmonious life amidst a tapestry of diverse cultures and experiences. And so, the story continues, a vibrant and ever-evolving narrative woven with threads of laughter, love, and the enduring spirit of a family that celebrates its differences. A family where the most beautiful music is the harmony of different voices, a testament to the power of love and acceptance, the true heart of our unconventional, yet remarkably beautiful, family.

The lessons on tolerance weren't confined to grand pronouncements or formal lectures. They were woven into the fabric of our daily lives, subtle yet potent, like the slow, steady drip of water shaping a stone. It started with the books we read. Liam, ever the voracious reader, discovered a passion for historical fiction, devouring stories of different eras and cultures. We encouraged this, supplementing his library with books featuring diverse characters and perspectives, ensuring he wasn't just reading about knights and dragons, but also about the struggles and triumphs of people from all walks of life. Chloe, with her artistic flair, found her own path to understanding through painting and drawing. Her canvases became vibrant expressions of different cultures, a testament to her burgeoning empathy and appreciation for the beauty of diversity.

One day, Liam came home from school visibly upset. A classmate had made a derogatory remark about his name, a name that held the weight of his heritage, a name that connected him to his ancestors. This presented a teachable moment that wasn't scripted, but organically sprung from the reality of their experience. We didn't shy away from the hurt; we acknowledged it, validated his feelings, and then engaged in a conversation about prejudice, its roots, and its impact. We explained the historical context of racial bias, the stereotypes that perpetuate prejudice, and the importance of challenging injustice when we see it. We talked about the power of words, and how they can build up or tear down. We encouraged him to articulate his feelings to his teacher and to his classmate, not with anger, but with a calm and assertive explanation of why the comment was hurtful and inappropriate.

This incident prompted a broader conversation about tolerance and acceptance, a conversation that extended to Chloe as well. We used the opportunity to talk about the importance of celebrating differences rather than fearing them, of recognizing the richness that diversity brings to our lives. We weren't preaching from some lofty moral high ground; we were sharing our own experiences, our own struggles with prejudice, and our own triumphs in overcoming adversity. We emphasized the importance of empathy, of trying to understand other people's perspectives, even when those perspectives differ greatly from our own.

Our efforts extended beyond our immediate family. We actively sought opportunities to expose our children to diverse perspectives, enrolling them in schools with diverse student populations and encouraging participation in community events that celebrated different cultures. We made conscious choices about our social circle, ensuring that our children were exposed to a wide range of people with different backgrounds, beliefs, and experiences. We took them to museums, art galleries, and cultural festivals, immersing them in the rich tapestry of human experience. And yes, there were awkward moments, misunderstandings, and sometimes even outright prejudice. But we used these moments as opportunities to learn, to grow, and to teach our children the importance of standing up for what is right.

One particularly memorable experience involved a school project where Liam had to create a presentation on a historical figure. He chose to focus on Nelson Mandela, a figure whose story resonated deeply with him. His presentation was not just a recitation of facts and dates; it was a passionate tribute to Mandela's resilience, his unwavering commitment to justice, and his profound impact on the world. The presentation touched his classmates, leading to thoughtful questions and stimulating discussions about apartheid, racial equality, and the importance of fighting for what you believe in. It wasn't just a school project; it was a powerful lesson in empathy, courage, and the transformative power of understanding.

We also taught our children the importance of self-acceptance and self-love, recognizing that genuine tolerance starts from within. We encouraged them to embrace their own unique identities, to celebrate their own strengths and weaknesses, and to develop a strong sense of self-worth. This wasn't about blind self-confidence, but a realistic understanding of their worth and the value they bring to the world. We instilled in them the idea that it's okay to be different, to stand out, and to embrace their unique blend of cultures and perspectives. It was crucial to nurture their individuality while also helping them understand the broader context of their identities within a diverse world.

This journey wasn't without its bumps and detours. There were times when Liam and Chloe faced challenges at school, encountering prejudice, misunderstandings, or exclusion. These moments weren't brushed aside, rather, we approached them with openness and frank discussion. We helped them understand their emotions, validated their feelings, and equipped them with the tools to navigate these situations with resilience and grace. It wasn't about shielding them from reality, but about empowering them to overcome adversity and make their voices heard.

Our family dinners became forums for ongoing conversations about tolerance and acceptance. We shared stories about our own experiences with prejudice, both large and small, encouraging our children to share their own observations and experiences. This open communication created a safe space where they felt comfortable expressing their thoughts and feelings, knowing that their concerns would be heard and acknowledged. The dinner table became more than just a place to eat; it transformed into a microcosm of the world, a space where we could explore different perspectives, celebrate our similarities, and learn from our differences. The conversations weren't always easy, sometimes leading to spirited debates and differing viewpoints, but the shared experience of respectfully engaging in dialogue became a powerful foundation for cultivating tolerance and mutual understanding.

The holidays, too, became opportunities for teaching tolerance. We celebrated both Hanukkah and Kwanzaa, not as separate occasions, but as intertwined celebrations of family, community, and cultural heritage. The children learned the meaning behind the traditions of both celebrations, developing an understanding and appreciation for their diverse origins. This blending of traditions wasn't forced; it was a natural extension of our family's diverse composition. It allowed them to grasp that traditions, while diverse, could coexist and even enhance each other.

But the most valuable lessons weren't delivered through lectures or grand pronouncements. They were conveyed through observation, emulation, and the subtle, everyday actions that demonstrated our values. They saw how Sarah and I, despite our different cultural backgrounds, navigated our relationship with mutual respect, understanding, and love. They witnessed how we addressed conflicts calmly and constructively, seeking common ground rather than succumbing to division. They learned that empathy is not simply a word, but a way of being, a disposition of mind that leads to understanding and compassion. They saw tolerance not as a passive acceptance of differences, but as an active engagement with the complexities of the world.

Our journey towards raising tolerant children wasn't a linear path; it was an ongoing process of learning, adaptation, and evolution. It required patience, understanding, and a constant willingness to challenge our own biases and prejudices. It wasn't about achieving some utopian ideal of perfect tolerance, but rather about continuously striving to create a culture of respect, empathy, and acceptance in our home and extending it outwards to the wider world. It was, and remains, a journey of discovery—a beautiful, imperfect, and endlessly rewarding journey that shapes not only our children but ourselves as well. The laughter, tears, and shared experiences along the way became the very essence of our family story, a testament to the power of love, acceptance, and the enduring strength of a blended family navigating the complexities of a diverse world. The ultimate lesson wasn't about tolerance alone, but about celebrating the kaleidoscope of cultures and perspectives that make our world so rich and vibrant.

The first Thanksgiving after Sarah and I married was... an experiment. My family, steeped in the soulful traditions of the South, brought collard greens, candied yams that practically glowed, and a macaroni and cheese so rich it could clog an artery from ten feet away. Sarah's family, Midwesterners through and through, countered with pumpkin pie the size of a small child, a mountain of mashed potatoes that could bury a small dog, and enough cranberry sauce to make a small cranberry farm jealous.

The initial clash of culinary styles was... entertaining. My Aunt Mildred, bless her heart, almost had a stroke trying to decipher the instructions on Sarah's grandmother's infamous "Grandma Betty's Ambrosia Salad," a concoction that involved marshmallows, canned fruit cocktail, and something suspiciously resembling Miracle Whip. It was a beautiful, chaotic mess, a culinary illustration of our merging lives.

Liam, ever the diplomat, declared both the collard greens and the pumpkin pie "delicious," though I caught him discreetly piling more mashed potatoes onto his plate. Chloe, with her artist's eye, took photos of the chaotic spread, her camera capturing the vibrant collision of flavors and traditions. That first Thanksgiving, far from being a disaster, was a hilarious, heart-warming beginning to a new family tradition.

Christmas was another story. My family's Christmas Eve included a gospel choir, a feast that stretched into the wee hours, and the exchange of gifts that were less about material possessions and more about heartfelt sentiment. Sarah's family, while equally loving, opted for a cozy evening by the fireplace, stockings hung with care, and a more restrained gift-giving ritual. The first Christmas together became a negotiation, a blend of both styles. We incorporated elements from both traditions: a shortened gospel performance (Aunt Mildred's suggestion—the choir had to get home for Midnight Mass), the cozy fireplace, and a gift exchange that balanced sentiment with a touch of festive extravagance.

The merging wasn't just about food and holidays; it impacted every aspect of our lives. We discovered that Sarah's family's Sunday morning pancake breakfasts could be elevated by the addition of my grandmother's secret pancake syrup recipe—a blend of maple syrup, bourbon, and a dash of cinnamon that could convert even the most ardent pancake skeptic. Liam and Chloe started participating in Sarah's family's annual summer lake-house vacation, introducing their newfound love for fishing to their cousins. They, in turn, taught Liam and Chloe the subtle art of water-skiing.

Our summer vacations transformed from predictable trips to my grandmother's home to a rotating roster of destinations that included national parks, historical sites, and beach towns. Liam and Chloe learned to appreciate both the quiet comforts of home and the excitement of exploring new places. It wasn't simply a compromise; it was a conscious decision to create new traditions, traditions that were uniquely ours.

We even tackled the complexities of birthdays. My family's celebrations were boisterous affairs, complete with impromptu karaoke sessions and enough cake to feed a small army. Sarah's family preferred quieter, more intimate gatherings. We learned to navigate this difference by having two celebrations: one for each family, allowing the children to enjoy the unique customs of both sides of their heritage.

This approach wasn't always smooth. There were moments of friction, misunderstandings, and even the occasional family feud. There was the infamous incident involving Aunt Mildred's attempt to teach Sarah's grandmother how to play dominoes (a game Sarah's grandmother deemed "too slow-paced"), and the time Uncle Joe tried to explain the nuances of college football to Sarah's father, who was a devout opera enthusiast. However, these conflicts, far from causing irreparable damage, often provided the basis for hilarious stories and a deeper understanding of each other's cultural backgrounds. They underscored the fact that embracing different traditions doesn't mean sacrificing one's own; rather, it's about creating a tapestry woven from different threads.

Even something as seemingly simple as bedtime stories evolved. Initially, Liam and Chloe would each receive stories reflecting their separate heritage. Gradually, we started incorporating stories from both cultures, introducing them to the richness and diversity of global storytelling. The children began to see the common threads weaving through seemingly disparate cultures, discovering the universal themes of love, loss, courage, and resilience that resonated across generations and geographical boundaries.

The evolution of our traditions wasn't merely a logistical exercise. It was a powerful demonstration of our commitment to creating a truly blended family. It was a testament to our ability to respect and value our differences while celebrating our shared love and commitment. It was about more than simply merging two sets of traditions; it was about forging a new path, a new identity as a family.

One particularly heartwarming moment occurred during Kwanzaa. Sarah's family, initially unfamiliar with the celebration, embraced it with open arms. They learned about the seven principles of Kwanzaa, the significance of the Kinara, and the importance of unity, self-determination, and collective responsibility. The children, fluent in both the traditions of Kwanzaa and Christmas, became the family's cultural ambassadors, enthusiastically explaining the meaning and significance of both celebrations. This cross-cultural exchange created a shared understanding and appreciation for the diverse celebrations that enriched our lives.

The blending of our traditions wasn't a perfect process; it was a work in progress, an ongoing evolution. There were times when old habits died hard, when the weight of tradition felt overwhelming. But through it all, we found laughter in the chaos, strength in our differences, and a deeper love in the shared experiences. The children, in turn, learned the valuable lesson of adaptability, understanding, and the inherent beauty in the fusion of cultures.

The evolving traditions became a reflection of our family's growth, a testament to our ability to embrace the complexities of our diverse backgrounds. It's a story of compromise, adaptation, and ultimately, a celebration of the rich mosaic of our lives. It's a testament to the fact that traditions, far from being static and immutable, are dynamic entities that adapt and evolve along with the families who cherish them.

The transformation wasn't just about adding new elements to our lives; it was about changing our perspectives. We learned to appreciate the nuances of each other's traditions, to understand the historical contexts that shaped them, and to find common ground in our shared values and aspirations. Our conversations extended beyond the dinner table, weaving their way into everyday interactions, shaping our perspectives, and strengthening the bond between us.

The evolution of our traditions is still ongoing. New customs are being developed, old ones are being reimagined, and the children are actively shaping the future of our family traditions. This ongoing process, marked by both laughter and occasional friction, is the very essence of our family story. It's a continuing narrative, a testament to the power of love, compromise, and the enduring spirit of a blended family embracing the vibrant tapestry of their interwoven heritage. It is a beautiful, chaotic, and endlessly rewarding journey. The journey of a family finding its unique rhythm, its own melody, in the harmonious discord of two distinct cultures becoming one. And that, in itself, is a tradition worth celebrating.

The ripple effect of our blended family extended far beyond our doorstep. It started subtly, with Liam and Chloe becoming unlikely ambassadors of cultural understanding in their school. Liam, once hesitant to share details of his Kwanzaa celebrations, found himself eagerly explaining the significance of the Kinara to his classmates, his words infused with newfound confidence. Chloe, equally enthusiastic, showcased her artistic talents by creating colourful depictions of both Christmas and Kwanzaa traditions for the school's holiday display, bridging the cultural gap with vibrant strokes of paint. Their classmates, initially curious and perhaps a little apprehensive, became captivated by the stories Liam and Chloe shared, their perspectives broadening with each shared experience. The school's annual multicultural festival became a vibrant showcase of our family's unique blend, with

Liam confidently leading a lively Kwanzaa presentation and Chloe's art becoming the centrepiece of the event. The children's genuine enthusiasm was contagious, transforming the festival from a mere school event into a community celebration.

Our influence seeped into the broader community through unexpected avenues. Sarah, a gifted baker, began incorporating elements of Southern soul food into her already impressive repertoire. Her famous apple pies now included a hint of bourbon, a subtle nod to my grandmother's secret ingredient. She started hosting baking workshops at the local community center, sharing both Midwestern classics and Southern comfort food recipes, fostering a spirit of cross-cultural exchange through the shared pleasure of baking. The workshops became a melting pot of cultures, a space where people from all backgrounds came together, united by their shared love of delicious treats.

My involvement in the local community theatre provided another platform for cultural bridging. Initially reluctant to include elements of African American culture in the productions, I found myself incorporating traditional songs and dances into our adaptations of classic plays, creating a rich tapestry of storytelling that reflected the diversity of our community. The inclusion of these elements not only enriched the productions but also sparked meaningful conversations among the actors, crew, and audience, challenging preconceived notions and fostering a greater appreciation for diverse artistic expressions. The positive response to these productions encouraged other community groups to embrace a more inclusive approach to their creative endeavors, expanding the scope of our community's artistic expression.

Even seemingly mundane activities, like our weekly family game nights, became a platform for cultural exchange. Sarah's family introduced us to the complexities of bridge, a game that, initially, I found bewilderingly intricate. My family, in turn, introduced them to the fast-paced excitement of Spades, a game that relied more on intuition than strategic planning. The competition was friendly, but fierce. These games, while seemingly trivial, fostered a sense of unity and understanding, as we learned each other's strategic styles and approaches. It provided an opportunity for deeper connection, understanding and appreciation for different ways of thinking and working together. These relaxed moments allowed for genuine cross-cultural exchange, stripping away barriers and fostering a deeper appreciation for each other's differences.

We found that our simple acts of daily life had a profound impact on the community. We actively participated in local charity events, supporting organizations dedicated to promoting racial harmony and cross-cultural understanding. Liam volunteered at the local library, assisting with their literacy programs, sharing his enthusiasm for storytelling with children from diverse backgrounds. Chloe, ever the artist, used her talent to create murals depicting scenes from diverse cultures, adding a splash of vibrant color and cultural richness to our community's landscape. The children's involvement in these activities fostered a sense of community responsibility and a genuine commitment to bridging the cultural divide. Their actions became a catalyst for social change, inspiring others to get involved and create a more inclusive and harmonious community.

Our family's impact was not merely the result of grand gestures; rather, it was the culmination of countless small acts of kindness, understanding, and inclusivity. The simple act of sharing a meal, engaging in a friendly game, participating in a community event, or simply engaging in open dialogue became a powerful force for social change. The very fabric of our blended family became a model for interracial harmony, demonstrating that bridging the cultural divide begins with the most fundamental human connection – the shared experiences and love within a family.

Our story wasn't about erasing differences; it was about celebrating them. It was about recognizing the strength and beauty found in the vibrant tapestry of our diverse backgrounds. It was about fostering empathy, building bridges of understanding, and creating a space where differences were not barriers, but rather a source of enrichment and growth. The journey wasn't always easy, filled with its share of misunderstandings and challenges. But it was the journey itself, this constant negotiation and adaptation, that cemented the strength of our bonds, forged a new family tradition, and demonstrated the power of a blended family to impact a community. It showed that creating a truly inclusive society is not a utopian ideal, but an achievable reality, one family, one community, one act of kindness at a time.

The children, witnessing our efforts and absorbing the lessons of cultural understanding, became active participants in this ongoing project. They weren't just passive recipients of our traditions; they were active architects of our family's unique cultural landscape. They navigated the complexities of their heritage with remarkable grace and ease, effortlessly blending the traditions of their mother and father, creating their own unique cultural identities that incorporated the best of both worlds. The way in which they seamlessly blended the rituals and celebrations of their diverse backgrounds became an inspiring example to others, demonstrating the power of inclusivity and acceptance.

This transformation didn't happen overnight; it was a gradual process that required patience, understanding, and a constant willingness to learn and adapt. There were times when tensions flared, when old prejudices surfaced, and when the weight of cultural differences felt overwhelming. Yet, through it all, laughter and love prevailed. Our journey was a testament to the power of resilience, the strength found in unity, and the beauty of a family embracing its diverse heritage.

Our story continues to unfold, ever evolving, ever expanding. Our family serves as a powerful reminder that bridging cultural divides is not merely a social obligation, but a deeply enriching human experience. It's about recognizing the shared humanity that binds us together, celebrating the unique beauty of our differences, and building a future where diversity is not a source of conflict, but a celebration of our collective strength and richness. Our family's story is a testament to the transformative power of love, understanding, and the enduring legacy of a blended family. It's a narrative that continues to be written, a chapter at a time, enriching both our lives and the lives of those around us, forging a path for a more inclusive and harmonious future. And that, perhaps, is the most significant and enduring tradition of all.

The annual family vacation, once a predictable rotation of beach trips or visits to Grandma's, morphed into something entirely new. Our first "blended" vacation to Charleston, South Carolina, was a masterclass in organized chaos. Sarah, ever the planner, had meticulously crafted an itinerary filled with historical tours, plantation visits, and elegant dinners. I, on the other hand, envisioned a more spontaneous adventure, punctuated by impromptu barbecues and spontaneous jam sessions. The children, bless their hearts, found themselves caught in the middle, expertly navigating the clash of our contrasting styles. Liam, ever the diplomat, suggested we split our time – half structured, half spontaneous – a compromise that surprisingly worked. We explored the city's rich history, marveling at the architecture and learning about its pivotal role in American history. Simultaneously, we discovered hidden gems – local soul food joints, lively blues clubs, and charming waterfront parks where we could relax and enjoy each other's company. The resulting blend created a vacation experience richer and more meaningful than either of us could have planned individually. It was a microcosm of our blended family – a beautiful tapestry woven from diverse threads, each adding its unique texture and colour.

The tension wasn't completely absent, of course. Sarah's family, accustomed to a certain level of refinement, occasionally expressed subtle (and sometimes not-so-subtle) disapproval of our more boisterous, less formal approach. My family, conversely, found Sarah's meticulous planning somewhat stifling, craving the freedom of spontaneous adventure. But the children, again, were the glue, adeptly mediating between their parents' contrasting styles. Liam's enthusiasm for history balanced Sarah's preference for structured tours, while Chloe's artistic eye captured the beauty of both Charleston's elegant architecture and the vibrant energy of its soul food restaurants. The children became our family's cultural translators, explaining their mother's family's emphasis on tradition and their father's more casual, improvisational approach to life. Their ability to bridge the gap between cultures became a source of pride for all of us.

Our Thanksgiving celebrations became a similarly fascinating blend of traditions. Sarah's family brought their classic Midwestern fare – pumpkin pie, roasted turkey, and all the comforting fixings. My family contributed our soul food staples – collard greens, mac and cheese, and sweet potato pie. The resulting feast was a testament to our family's unique heritage, a delicious collision of flavors and culinary traditions. The children, rather than feeling overwhelmed by the sheer abundance of food, eagerly embraced the culinary adventure, their plates a reflection of our diverse heritage. The discussions around the table, a mix of polite conversation and boisterous laughter, showcased the rich tapestry of our family's history, our differing perspectives enriching rather than detracting from the overall experience. We found a way to celebrate both traditions without compromising our individual identities. It wasn't about assimilation; it was about integration – a beautiful blending of cultures, a testament to the strength and resilience of our blended family.

Christmas followed a similar pattern. We decorated the Christmas tree with both traditional ornaments and handmade decorations crafted by Chloe, reflecting elements of both our cultural backgrounds. We exchanged gifts, shared stories, and engaged in both quiet moments of reflection and boisterous games. The children embraced the festive spirit with unbridled enthusiasm, their joy infectious. The Christmas carols we sang echoed with the diverse melodies of our heritage. We even incorporated elements of Kwanzaa into our celebrations, explaining its significance to Sarah's family and learning more about their holiday traditions in return. It wasn't about replacing one tradition with another, but about layering them, creating a richer, more complex celebration that truly reflected our family's unique identity.

Even the seemingly mundane aspects of daily life took on a new significance. Dinner conversations, once a casual exchange of daily events, became rich discussions about history, culture, and current events. We explored different perspectives, challenging our assumptions and expanding our understanding of each other. The children actively participated in these conversations, sharing their experiences at school and offering their unique insights. The shared meals, once a simple act of sustenance, became a ritual of cultural exchange, an opportunity to learn from each other and appreciate our diverse backgrounds. The simple act of sharing a meal transformed into a powerful symbol of our family's unity.

Over time, we developed new family traditions that uniquely reflected our multicultural heritage. We celebrated both Christmas and Kwanzaa, blending elements of both traditions to create a unique holiday experience. We incorporated soul food and Midwestern dishes into our weekly meal plans, creating a culinary fusion that delighted everyone's palates. Our summer vacations became a mix of historical explorations and spontaneous adventures, offering a balanced approach to family travel. The children actively participated in creating these traditions, adding their own unique ideas and perspectives. This process of collaborative creation helped shape our family's identity, creating a sense of belonging and shared purpose. They weren't just blending traditions; they were building a new, vibrant family culture.

The journey wasn't without its bumps in the road. There were moments of frustration, misunderstandings, and even conflict. But through it all, our love for each other and our unwavering commitment to building a strong, inclusive family proved to be a powerful force. We learned to communicate openly and honestly, to listen to each other's perspectives, and to appreciate the richness of our differences. We discovered that our differences, once a source of conflict, could become a source of strength and resilience. We weren't just a family; we were a community, a microcosm of the world we aspired to live in – a world where diversity was celebrated, not feared.

The culmination of this journey was a profound sense of acceptance, not just from within our family but from our wider community as well. We had become a beacon of interracial harmony, inspiring others to embrace the beauty of diversity. Our children, raised in a home where differences were celebrated, became confident, compassionate, and understanding individuals. They were living proof that a blended family could thrive, could create a new normal, could even redefine what "normal" means in a world obsessed with conformity. They demonstrated that differences weren't obstacles to overcome, but opportunities to enrich and enhance our lives. Their acceptance of their heritage, and their embrace of the blending of two vastly different cultures, became a testament to the resilience of the human spirit and the power of love to transcend differences.

Our "new normal" wasn't about erasing our differences; it was about celebrating them, embracing the rich tapestry of our diverse backgrounds, and weaving a new, vibrant pattern of family life. It was about creating a space where everyone felt valued, respected, and loved, regardless of their race, culture, or background. It was a testament to the strength of our love, our commitment to each other, and the remarkable ability of a family to adapt, to evolve, and to create its own unique definition of happiness. And in that, we found a profound and enduring sense of peace, a sense of belonging, a sense of home. The laughter, the shared meals, the spontaneous adventures – these were the building blocks of our new normal, a testament to the enduring power of love and acceptance in a world that often struggles to find both. The new normal wasn't just a state of being; it was a journey, a continuous evolution of love, understanding and the unwavering commitment to creating a space where diversity thrived.

Chapter 6: Lessons Learned

Looking back, it's easy to romanticize the whirlwind romance that swept Sarah and me off our feet. The fairy tale wedding, the adorable blended family portraits – they all make for a lovely slideshow, the kind you'd show off at a particularly upbeat family reunion. But the reality? The reality was a messy, hilarious, occasionally heartbreaking, and ultimately triumphant journey through uncharted territory. We weren't just navigating the choppy waters of a new marriage; we were charting a course across a vast, unmapped ocean of cultural differences, societal expectations, and deeply ingrained prejudices.

One of the biggest hurdles, ironically, wasn't the blatant racism – though we certainly encountered our share of that. It was the subtle, insidious kind of prejudice, the microaggressions that chipped away at our confidence, the sidelong glances, the hushed whispers, the assumptions based solely on appearances. There were times when Sarah would be mistaken for my nanny, or I would be asked, with a patronizing smile, "So, how did *you* meet *her*?" These little barbs, seemingly insignificant on their own, accumulated like tiny pebbles, slowly building a wall between us and the world.

We learned, early on, the importance of having each other's backs. We developed a silent language, a shared glance, a subtle touch that communicated volumes without uttering a word. We became each other's refuge, our safe harbor in a sea of judgment. We were a team, a united front against the undercurrent of disapproval. We'd laugh it off, we'd strategize, we'd even make inside jokes out of the absurd situations we found ourselves in. Turning the discomfort into humor became a vital coping mechanism, defusing potentially explosive situations with a well-timed quip or a shared knowing smile. Humor, it turned out, was our secret weapon.

Navigating family dynamics proved equally challenging. Sarah's family, steeped in Midwestern traditions and a certain level of polite formality, often struggled to understand my family's more boisterous, expressive style. Conversely, my family, accustomed to a more casual and spontaneous approach to life, found Sarah's meticulous planning a bit stifling. It wasn't about right or wrong; it was about different ways of being, different expressions of love and connection. The key, we discovered, wasn't to erase our differences, but to learn to appreciate and even celebrate them.

We found ourselves constantly negotiating, compromising, finding common ground. It was a constant process of give-and-take, of learning to understand each other's perspectives, of acknowledging and respecting each other's needs. There were times when we stumbled, when frustration boiled over, when we found ourselves on opposite sides of a chasm. But those moments, painful as they were, became opportunities for growth, for deeper understanding, for a stronger, more resilient bond. We learned to articulate our feelings, to express our needs, to listen to each other with genuine empathy. We learned that effective communication wasn't about winning an argument; it was about building bridges.

The children, of course, were instrumental in our journey. They were the silent mediators, the unsung heroes who navigated the complexities of our blended family with remarkable grace and understanding. They effortlessly blended our contrasting traditions, embodying the spirit of unity and understanding that we strived for. They were, in many ways, our teachers. They taught us patience, acceptance, and the importance of unconditional love. They showed us that different doesn't mean wrong; it simply means different.

One unexpected obstacle was the burden of representation. We found ourselves, quite unintentionally, becoming symbols of interracial harmony. People looked to us, judged us, projected their own hopes and fears onto our family. There were times when the weight of those expectations felt overwhelming. We learned to protect ourselves, to set boundaries, to choose our battles. We realized that we couldn't be everything to everyone, and that it was okay to prioritize our own well-being and happiness.

Overcoming these challenges wasn't a linear progression. It was a series of steps forward, followed by occasional stumbles backward. There were times when we doubted ourselves, when we questioned whether we could make this work. But through it all, our love for each other, our commitment to our family, served as our unwavering compass. We learned to rely on each other, to support each other, to cherish each other, even amidst the chaos and confusion.

Our friends and extended families also played an essential role. Slowly, gradually, with patience and understanding, many began to see beyond the initial shock and awe, beyond the preconceived notions and stereotypes. They came to appreciate the richness and diversity of our blended family. They witnessed our love, our commitment, and the deep affection we shared. They saw our children thriving, secure, and happy. And that, ultimately, was the most powerful testimony to the success of our unconventional family.

This wasn't about changing the world overnight, about magically erasing prejudice. It was about making a difference in our own small corner of it. It was about showing the world that a blended family, a multiracial family, could thrive, could flourish, could be a source of joy, love, and unwavering support. It was a testament to the power of love and acceptance, a beacon of hope in a world often defined by its divisions. And most importantly, it was a journey of self-discovery, of growth, and of unwavering commitment to building a life filled with laughter, love, and a healthy dose of perfectly chaotic family adventures. We became living, breathing proof that a new normal was not just possible, but beautiful. It wasn't about conformity; it was about creating a unique tapestry woven from the threads of our diverse experiences, a tapestry that, though sometimes frayed at the edges, was ultimately beautiful and strong. And that, my friends, is a story worth telling, a story worth celebrating. The journey itself, with all its bumps and detours, became the most profound lesson of all. The obstacles we faced, the challenges we overcame, only served to strengthen the bonds that held us together. They taught us resilience, adaptability, and the enduring power of love to conquer all. And somewhere amidst the laughter, the tears, and the occasional family feud, we found our happy ever after. It wasn't the fairy tale we initially imagined, but it was a story far more beautiful, far more real, and far more meaningful. And that's the story of how we learned to love, to laugh, and to live, even when life threw us its most challenging curveballs. The lessons weren't just learned; they were lived, breathed, and celebrated. And that's a story worth sharing.

But the laughter, the shared jokes, the inside quips born from the absurdity of it all—that was the glue. That was the unexpected strength that held us together, a testament to the resilience of our love. It wasn't just a romantic love; it was a partnership, a fierce alliance forged in the fires of societal judgment and familial misunderstandings. We learned to anticipate each other's needs, to finish each other's sentences, not just with words, but with actions, with a knowing glance that said, "I've got your back."

This wasn't some Hallmark movie; it was real life, messy and chaotic, a comedy of errors played out on the grand stage of our interracial, blended family. There were screaming matches in the kitchen, tears shed in quiet corners, moments of doubt that gnawed at our souls. We argued about everything – from the best way to cook collard greens (Sarah's delicate approach versus my grandma's "throw it all in and hope for the best" method) to the merits of different holiday traditions. But even in the midst of these disagreements, our love remained the unshakeable foundation. It was the anchor that kept us from drifting too far apart, the compass that guided us back to each other whenever we veered off course.

The power of our love wasn't just felt by us; it was palpable to those around us. Slowly, hesitantly at first, the initial resistance from both sides of our families began to melt away. Sarah's initially reserved Midwestern relatives came to appreciate the warmth and exuberance of my Southern family, witnessing firsthand their genuine affection and unwavering support. My family, initially wary of Sarah's reserved nature, saw beyond the initial polite façade, discovering a woman of incredible strength, resilience, and unwavering devotion. They saw how she handled the challenges with grace, her love for me and our children shining through every interaction.

The children, our beautiful, blended brood, became the ultimate ambassadors of love and acceptance. They navigated the complexities of two distinct cultures with an effortless grace, blending traditions and celebrating differences. They were the living embodiment of our union, a testament to the beauty of diversity and the power of family. They taught us, more than we could ever have imagined, the true meaning of unconditional love and acceptance. They showed us that love doesn't conform to societal norms; it creates its own, unique and beautiful, reality.

Our friends, too, were crucial in this journey. Those who truly valued our relationship learned to see beyond the superficial differences, to embrace the richness of our diverse backgrounds. They celebrated our milestones, offered support during our struggles, and became an integral part of our extended family. Their acceptance wasn't just a passive nod; it was an active participation in our story, a testament to the power of friendship and the importance of choosing to see beyond societal prejudices.

This wasn't a fairy tale; it was a testament to the enduring power of love in the face of adversity. It was a battle fought and won, not on the battlefield of social norms, but on the intimate grounds of our own hearts and homes. We didn't change the world; we changed our little corner of it, one laughter-filled dinner, one heartfelt conversation, one shared glance at a time. We didn't erase prejudice; we created a haven where it held no power, a sanctuary of love that radiated outward, touching those around us.

The power of love, in our case, wasn't a magical force that erased conflict or instantly resolved every disagreement. It was a constant, active choice. It was the choice to communicate openly and honestly, even when it was uncomfortable. It was the choice to forgive, to understand, to compromise, even when it felt impossible. It was the choice to fight for our relationship, for our family, for our future. It was the choice to acknowledge our differences, celebrate our uniqueness, and find strength in our shared vulnerabilities.

The lessons we learned weren't always pleasant, but they were invaluable. We learned the importance of communication, not just the words we spoke, but the silent language of understanding and empathy that transcended words. We learned the power of forgiveness, the ability to let go of anger and resentment, and move forward with love as our guiding light. We learned the art of compromise, the willingness to meet each other halfway, to understand different perspectives, even when those perspectives challenged our own.

We learned the importance of self-care, of prioritizing our own well-being, so we could be the best versions of ourselves for our family. We learned that it's okay to set boundaries, to protect our emotional space, to choose our battles wisely. We learned the value of laughter, the ability to find humor in the chaos, to use humor as a tool to diffuse tense situations and to create a lighter atmosphere. We learned that love isn't always easy, and that's okay.

Our love story is not a fairy tale; it's a testament to the human spirit's capacity for resilience, understanding, and growth. It's a story of two people from vastly different backgrounds, who defied expectations, challenged societal norms, and created a beautiful, thriving family despite the odds. It's a story about the power of love to overcome prejudice, to bridge cultural divides, and to build a life filled with laughter, love, and unwavering support. It's a story that demonstrates that love, in all its messy, complicated glory, is the most powerful force in the world. It's a force that can heal wounds, mend broken hearts, and inspire hope, even in the face of overwhelming adversity.

And it's a story that's still unfolding, filled with ongoing challenges and unexpected joys, but always grounded in the unshakeable foundation of our love. It's a testament to the power of perseverance, a celebration of the beautiful tapestry of our unconventional family, and an ongoing testament to the power of love to conquer all. It's a story of learning, growing, and loving unconditionally, even when it's messy, challenging, and utterly hilarious. It's a story worth sharing, a story worth celebrating, a story worth living. Because in the end, it's not the absence of conflict but the strength of our love that defines us, a love that has transformed obstacles into opportunities, challenges into triumphs, and differences into a beautiful, vibrant, and unforgettable family. And that, my friends, is a love story worth telling. A story that reminds us all that love can indeed conquer all. A story that continues, one hilarious, heartwarming, and incredibly challenging chapter at a time.

But the cornerstone of our success, the bedrock upon which our unconventional family was built, was undeniably communication. It wasn't just about the words we exchanged, the daily pleasantries, or the occasional heated debate over whose turn it was to do the dishes (a surprisingly contentious topic in our household). It was about the unspoken language, the subtle cues, the shared glances that spoke volumes more than any carefully crafted sentence. It was about truly listening, not just hearing.

It took time. Initially, our communication was a battlefield. Sarah, raised in a household where emotions were carefully curated and disagreements were politely swept under the rug, struggled with my family's more expressive, often boisterous, communication style. My family, accustomed to direct and sometimes blunt communication, found Sarah's reserved nature initially perplexing. We were two ships passing in the night, each speaking a different language. Arguments erupted, fueled by misunderstandings born from differing communication styles, cultural nuances, and ingrained expectations. We'd find ourselves tangled in a web of misinterpretations, each of us feeling unheard, unvalidated, and ultimately misunderstood.

One particularly memorable incident involved Sarah's attempt to make collard greens. Having grown up on her mother's delicate, almost dainty, version of the Southern staple, she tried to replicate it, resulting in a pot of limp, pale green leaves that tasted suspiciously like sadness. My family, accustomed to Grandma Millie's hearty, robust collard greens – a culinary experience akin to a small-scale earthquake – reacted with stunned silence, followed by a chorus of sympathetic groans and thinly veiled criticisms. Sarah, devastated by the lackluster reception, retreated, hurt and confused. It wasn't just about the collard greens; it was about the clash of culinary cultures, the difference in expectations, and a fundamental misunderstanding of communication styles.

It wasn't until I sat down with Sarah, gently explaining the nuances of my family's communication style – the boisterous expressions of affection, the seemingly harsh critiques masked by underlying care, the importance of hearty, almost defiant, food – that the situation began to shift. I explained that their criticisms weren't personal attacks, but rather a demonstration of their high standards and affection. They'd expect more if they didn't care about you. We used a similar approach when we interacted with Sarah's family.

Similarly, I had to learn to decipher Sarah's more subtle cues. Her quiet silences weren't necessarily signs of disapproval, but rather a reflection of her processing things internally. Her polite, almost hesitant, suggestions weren't expressions of weakness, but carefully considered opinions. Learning to recognize these subtle differences in communication transformed our relationship from one of constant friction to a carefully choreographed dance.

We started practicing active listening. We learned to truly focus on what the other person was saying, not just waiting for our turn to speak. We asked clarifying questions, repeated back what we heard to ensure understanding, and validated each other's feelings, even if we didn't always agree with their perspectives. We discovered that communication wasn't merely a vehicle for exchanging information, but a powerful tool for building empathy, fostering trust, and strengthening our bond. We practiced the art of 'I' statements, focusing on expressing our own feelings and needs without blaming or accusing the other person. "I feel hurt when…" was far more effective than "You always…"

This journey wasn't linear; it was a zigzagging, often bumpy, road filled with detours, wrong turns, and plenty of frustrating moments. There were times when our communication faltered, when misunderstandings resurfaced, and when the unspoken tensions simmered beneath the surface. But the commitment to open and honest communication, to working through conflicts rather than avoiding them, became the defining characteristic of our relationship. We learned that even the most difficult conversations were essential to growth, to intimacy, and ultimately, to the strength of our love.

This newfound understanding extended beyond our immediate relationship. It helped bridge the chasm between our families. We learned to translate between the communication styles of our respective families, acting as mediators, interpreters, and cultural ambassadors. Slowly, grudgingly at first, families who had once stared at each other with suspicion began to understand each other, to appreciate their differences, and to recognize the shared human experience that bound them together. The laughter, the shared meals, the clumsy attempts at cross-cultural understanding, all contributed to a new level of empathy and connection.

The children, bless their hearts, became masters of this intricate communication ballet. They navigated the complexities of two distinct cultures with an effortless grace, effortlessly switching between languages, traditions, and customs. They demonstrated a flexibility and adaptability that was a testament to the power of communication and the importance of understanding diverse perspectives. They were living proof that communication wasn't just about words; it was about connection, respect, and empathy. They demonstrated this, not just in words, but in their actions; the way they readily embraced different cuisines, different traditions, different ways of expressing love.

The ability to communicate effectively wasn't simply a skill we learned; it was a muscle we built, strengthened with each conversation, each compromise, each act of listening. It became an integral part of our daily lives, permeating every aspect of our interactions, transforming the way we interacted not just with each other but with the world around us. The power of communication allowed us to create a space where differences were celebrated, where conflicts were resolved with grace, and where love and understanding flourished. It transformed our family from a collection of individuals into a cohesive, supportive, and deeply loving unit. A family that thrived not despite our differences, but because of them. A family that understood the true meaning of communication, in all its messy, hilarious, and profoundly beautiful complexity.

This wasn't just about avoiding conflict; it was about understanding the root causes of disagreement. Often, our arguments stemmed not from malicious intent but from differing perspectives, unmet needs, and misunderstandings. Learning to identify these underlying issues became crucial in finding mutually agreeable solutions. It wasn't about winning or losing; it was about finding common ground, about building a bridge across the chasm of different viewpoints.

And the rewards were immeasurable. The ability to communicate effectively transformed our relationship from a source of stress to a sanctuary of mutual understanding and support. The trust we cultivated through open communication fostered deeper intimacy, a sense of connection that transcended words. The laughter, the shared experiences, the victories, and even the setbacks, were all woven together by a common thread: our commitment to honest and respectful communication.

It's a journey, not a destination. The challenges continue, but the tools we developed – the willingness to listen, the commitment to empathy, the relentless pursuit of understanding – remain our steadfast companions. We continue to learn, to grow, to communicate, and to love, each day a testament to the enduring power of open communication in building a strong and thriving family. Our story isn't a fairytale; it's a messy, hilarious, often challenging, but ultimately heartwarming, testament to the power of communication, compromise, and unwavering love.

But the tapestry of our lives didn't just weave together through effective communication; it blossomed with the vibrant threads of diversity. Sarah's family, steeped in the traditions of a different cultural background, brought a richness to our lives that I never could have imagined. Their quiet evenings filled with board games and thoughtful conversations were a stark contrast to my family's boisterous gatherings, echoing with laughter and the aroma of Grandma Millie's legendary collard greens (a culinary experience Sarah, bless her heart, was still attempting to master). This difference wasn't a source of conflict, but a source of fascination, a chance to learn and grow.

We explored different cuisines together. Sarah introduced us to delicate French pastries and elegant pasta dishes, while I countered with spicy jerk chicken and soul-stirring gumbo. Our dinner table became a culinary adventure, a vibrant reflection of our diverse heritage. The children, with the adaptability only children possess, navigated this culinary landscape with gusto, their palates as diverse as their cultural backgrounds. They were a testament to the beauty of cultural fusion, a living embodiment of the richness that comes from embracing different traditions.

We celebrated holidays in unique ways. Christmas mornings weren't just about stockings and Santa; they involved the quiet unwrapping of gifts in the morning followed by a festive gathering with Sarah's family, filled with carols and warm wishes. Thanksgiving, usually a whirlwind of family gatherings on my side, was tempered by Sarah's preference for a smaller, more intimate gathering focused on meaningful conversation and heartfelt gratitude. We learned to appreciate the nuances of each tradition, to blend them into a unique tapestry of celebration, creating memories that were both personal and uniquely ours.

Music became another bridge across our cultural divide. Sarah's family introduced us to the soothing melodies of classical music and the soulful sounds of jazz. My family countered with the upbeat rhythms of gospel music and the soulful lyrics of blues. Our home was filled with a rich tapestry of sounds, each note a testament to our diverse musical heritage. The children, ever adaptable, effortlessly absorbed these different musical styles, their musical tastes as diverse as their cultural backgrounds.

Art became another way we celebrated our diversity. We visited museums, admiring masterpieces from different cultures and eras. Sarah introduced us to the delicate brushstrokes of Impressionist paintings, while I shared my appreciation for the vibrant colors and bold lines of African American art. We discovered that art transcended cultural boundaries, its beauty capable of uniting us across differences.

The children, in turn, discovered their own artistic talents, expressing their individuality through a diverse array of creative endeavors, mirroring the richness of our family life.

Even seemingly mundane activities became opportunities to celebrate our diversity. Shopping trips involved exploring different stores, sampling diverse foods, and experiencing different retail cultures. Weekends might include visiting different neighborhoods, each with its unique character and history. These seemingly simple activities transformed into adventures, broadening our perspectives and enriching our understanding of the world around us. The children became cultural explorers, their curiosity piqued by the diverse experiences we shared.

Education became a key element in our journey towards embracing diversity. We intentionally sought out educational opportunities that exposed our children to different cultures and perspectives. We read books, watched documentaries, and participated in cultural events that broadened their understanding of the world. We enrolled them in schools that reflected the diversity of our community, encouraging them to interact with children from various backgrounds. This conscious effort to educate our children about diversity instilled in them a deep appreciation for cultural differences and the importance of inclusivity.

But the journey wasn't always smooth sailing. There were moments of awkwardness, of misunderstandings, and of cultural clashes. There were times when we struggled to navigate the complexities of our diverse backgrounds. However, these challenges never defined us. Instead, they became opportunities for learning, for growth, and for strengthening our bonds as a family. We learned to embrace the challenges, to view them as stepping stones on our path towards understanding and acceptance.

We learned to laugh at our mistakes, to find humor in our misunderstandings. We learned to celebrate the beauty of our differences, to see them not as sources of conflict, but as sources of strength and enrichment. We learned to value the perspectives of others, to broaden our understanding of the world. We learned to appreciate the richness that diversity brings to our lives, both on a personal level and on a societal level.

This understanding extended beyond our immediate family. We actively sought out opportunities to engage with people from diverse backgrounds, breaking down barriers and promoting inclusivity within our community. We participated in community events, volunteered at organizations that served diverse populations, and actively engaged in conversations about social justice and equality. We became advocates for diversity, using our experiences and our platform to promote a more inclusive and equitable society.

Our journey toward embracing diversity wasn't just a personal one; it was a social one. It involved confronting societal biases and prejudices, challenging stereotypes, and working towards a more just and equitable world. We learned that true inclusivity requires action, not just words. It requires a willingness to listen, to learn, and to challenge ourselves and others to be better. It requires a deep commitment to creating a world where everyone feels valued, respected, and empowered.

This journey of embracing diversity continues to unfold, enriching our lives in countless ways. Our family has become a living testament to the beauty of multiculturalism, a reflection of the richness and complexity of human experience. Our story is not just about a blended family; it's about the journey toward creating a more inclusive and harmonious world, one filled with laughter, love, and the vibrant tapestry of human diversity. The laughter, the understanding, the shared experiences – these were the true treasures, forged in the crucible of cultural exchange. And the children? They were the living embodiment of that fusion, the future of a world where differences are celebrated, not feared. A world where diversity isn't just tolerated, but cherished. A world where every voice has the chance to be heard, every culture valued, every individual celebrated. That, more than anything, is the enduring legacy of our family's story. A story that continues to unfold, each chapter filled with the vibrant colors of diversity, each page a testament to the power of love, understanding, and the unwavering belief in the inherent beauty of our differences.

But the question lingered, a quiet hum beneath the surface of our daily laughter and shared meals: What kind of legacy were we building? Were we merely creating a quirky, multi-cultural family album, or were we forging something deeper, something that could resonate beyond our immediate circle? The answer, we realized, lay not just in the memories we created, but in the values we instilled.

We wanted our children to grow up understanding that differences weren't obstacles, but opportunities. That the world wasn't a monochrome canvas, but a vibrant tapestry woven with a thousand threads of color, culture, and perspective. We didn't want them to simply tolerate diversity; we wanted them to embrace it, to celebrate it, to see it as a source of strength and enrichment.

This meant more than just sharing holiday traditions or experimenting with different cuisines. It meant actively engaging with the world around us, seeking out opportunities to learn about different cultures and perspectives. It meant traveling, not just as tourists, but as cultural explorers, immersing ourselves in the richness of different societies. We took them to historical sites, not just to memorize dates and facts, but to understand the human stories that shaped those places, the struggles and triumphs of diverse communities. We attended cultural festivals, not just as passive observers, but as active participants, embracing the music, the dance, the food, and the traditions. We encouraged them to learn new languages, not just as academic pursuits, but as keys to unlocking different cultures and perspectives.

Our home became a microcosm of the world we envisioned. Bookshelves overflowed with stories from around the globe, their pages filled with characters from different backgrounds, facing diverse challenges and celebrating varied triumphs. Our conversations weren't limited to our immediate experiences; they stretched to encompass global issues, from climate change to social justice, encouraging critical thinking and a sense of global citizenship. We didn't shy away from difficult discussions, embracing the complexities of the world, acknowledging its flaws while celebrating its inherent beauty. We wanted them to understand that the world wasn't perfect, but that it held immense potential for good, and that they could be a part of shaping that future.

We also emphasized the importance of empathy and understanding. We encouraged them to listen to different perspectives, even those that challenged their own beliefs. We fostered open dialogue, creating a safe space where they could express their thoughts and feelings without fear of judgment. We taught them the value of critical thinking, urging them to question assumptions and challenge stereotypes. We didn't shy away from difficult conversations about race, class, and social justice, equipping them with the tools to navigate a complex and often challenging world. We wanted them to be informed, engaged citizens, capable of navigating the complexities of a diverse society with grace and understanding.

This wasn't a passive process. It was an ongoing conversation, a continuous journey of learning and growth, both for us and for our children. There were moments of frustration, moments of misunderstanding, moments when we questioned our own approaches. But we persevered, driven by our belief in the power of diversity and the importance of leaving a positive legacy for future generations.

We found unexpected allies in our journey. Teachers, mentors, friends from diverse backgrounds – all helped to shape our children's understanding of the world. They provided different perspectives, challenged assumptions, and broadened our horizons. These relationships enriched our lives immeasurably, proving that the tapestry of our legacy was being woven by a multitude of hands, hearts, and minds.

Our legacy wasn't solely defined by grand gestures or monumental achievements. It was found in the small moments, the everyday interactions, the subtle shifts in perspective. It was in the laughter shared around the dinner table, the stories told at bedtime, the quiet moments of connection. It was in the way our children approached the world, with curiosity, empathy, and a deep appreciation for the richness of human diversity.

It wasn't always easy. There were moments of doubt, moments when the weight of our responsibilities felt overwhelming. But we clung to our vision, fueled by our love for our children and our belief in a better future. We saw our children not just as individuals, but as agents of change, the future architects of a more inclusive and equitable world. We hoped to equip them with the tools to build that world, to be the kind of leaders who would champion diversity and fight for social justice.

We recognized that our legacy wouldn't be solely defined by our family's story. Our family was a living testament to the possibilities of a diverse and interconnected world. It was a microcosm of a larger movement, a reflection of a growing societal awareness of the importance of diversity, equity, and inclusion. Our role was not simply to create a loving and supportive home for our children, but to actively contribute to a society that embraced these values.

We understood that the work wasn't finished. Our journey was ongoing; the legacy we were building was still under construction. Each day was an opportunity to reinforce the values we held dear, to model the behavior we hoped to see in our children, and to contribute to a world where everyone felt valued, respected, and empowered.

Our commitment to building this legacy was not confined to our family. We actively sought out opportunities to make a positive impact on the wider community. We volunteered at organizations that promoted diversity and social justice. We supported initiatives that aimed to bridge cultural divides and promote understanding. We used our platform to amplify the voices of marginalized communities and to advocate for policies that promoted equity and inclusion. We participated in community dialogues and discussions, challenging stereotypes and promoting respectful engagement with people from diverse backgrounds.

The legacy we hoped to leave wasn't just about our family's history; it was about inspiring others to build their own legacies of inclusion and understanding. We knew that our efforts wouldn't erase centuries of prejudice and inequality overnight. But we believed in the power of small acts, the ripple effect of positive change, and the cumulative impact of countless individuals working together to create a more just and equitable world.

Ultimately, the legacy we envisioned wasn't about perfection or achieving some predetermined goal. It was about the journey itself, the constant striving for improvement, the unwavering commitment to creating a world where diversity was not just tolerated, but celebrated, where differences were embraced, and where every individual had the opportunity to thrive. It was about instilling in our children a sense of responsibility, a commitment to social justice, and a profound belief in the power of human connection to overcome divisions and build a brighter future for all. The laughter, the tears, the struggles, the triumphs – all of it contributed to the rich tapestry of our family's story, a story that we hoped would inspire future generations to build their own legacies of love, understanding, and unwavering commitment to a world where everyone truly belongs. A world where our differences are not just tolerated, but treasured, celebrated, and ultimately, the very foundation of a richer, more vibrant future. A future where the laughter of our children, echoing the harmony of diverse voices, would be the most beautiful song of our legacy.

Chapter 7: Holiday Harmony (Almost)

The Christmas tree, a majestic fir, stood proudly in our living room, a testament to our ambitious—some might say delusional—attempt at a truly multicultural Christmas. It was adorned not only with the traditional twinkling lights and silver ornaments, but also with hand-painted Kwanzaa kinara, delicate origami stars from Japan, and miniature dreidels spinning precariously amongst the baubles. Beneath it, a chaotic jumble of presents hinted at the diverse origins of our family and friends.

My stepmother, bless her ambitious heart, had decided that this year would be the year we embraced *all* of our holiday traditions. The result was a holiday extravaganza that threatened to overwhelm even the most seasoned celebrant. First, there was the Christmas Eve dinner, a culinary fusion experiment gone slightly awry. My family's traditional Southern fried chicken clashed spectacularly with her family's traditional roast goose, a culinary mismatch that resulted in a table laden with a bewildering array of dishes, each vying for attention. My mother, a woman who considered burnt toast a culinary catastrophe, stared at the goose with a look of quiet horror, while my stepmother's mother, a woman whose culinary adventures typically involved meticulously crafted French pastries, cautiously sampled the fried chicken with a skeptical air.

The children, however, were in their element. They flitted between the dishes, sampling everything with the gusto only children possess, creating a happy, if slightly chaotic, culinary carnival. Their enthusiasm, however, failed to mask the underlying tension. My mother, a stickler for tradition, muttered darkly about the "lack of proper gravy" and the "unacceptable level of spice" in the collard greens. My stepmother's mother, meanwhile, discreetly removed the slightly charred bits from the goose, muttering about "rustic charm," which I suspected was code for "almost inedible."

The aftermath of the dinner was a culinary battlefield. Dishes piled high in the sink, the remnants of a feast that was both magnificent and mildly terrifying. But it was merely the prelude to the main event – the actual Christmas morning.

This involved a staggered unwrapping of gifts, a process complicated by different cultural approaches to gift-giving. My family, notoriously enthusiastic and effusive, launched into a joyous unwrapping frenzy. My stepmother's family, more reserved and refined, approached the ritual with a quiet dignity that bordered on the glacial. My children, caught between these two wildly different approaches, bounced between the two groups, their excitement a vibrant contrast to the controlled enthusiasm of their grandparents.

The gift-giving itself was a comedy of errors. My mother, deeply offended by what she considered a "lackluster" gift from my stepmother's mother (a hand-knitted scarf, impeccably crafted but, in my mother's opinion, utterly devoid of pizazz), launched into a lengthy monologue about the relative merits of hand-knitted versus machine-knitted scarves. My stepmother's mother, responding with the understated politeness of someone who had spent decades navigating the complexities of British high society, offered a polite, if slightly strained, smile.

Then there was the question of Christmas carols. My family's gusto in belting out traditional gospel carols clashed rather dramatically with my stepmother's family's preference for quiet, contemplative hymns. The result was a rather jarring musical experience, a sort of unholy alliance of joyful shouting and subdued humming that left everyone a little bewildered.

Kwanzaa, which we celebrated a few days later, was an entirely different affair. The Kinara, seven candles representing seven principles, glowed brightly against the backdrop of our living room. The children, armed with their homemade cards and gifts, presented them to their grandparents with a seriousness that belied their age. This was a ceremony, a reflection, a celebration of values – quite unlike the rather chaotic gift exchange of Christmas.

Hanukkah, surprisingly, flowed smoothly into the Kwanzaa celebrations. My stepmother's family seemed surprisingly adaptable; the lighting of the menorah blended in seamlessly with the lighting of the Kinara, the festive atmosphere somehow accommodating the simultaneous celebrations. The children, always quick to grasp opportunities for more presents, gleefully accepted the small gifts associated with each night of Hanukkah.

The entire holiday season was a dizzying whirl of traditions and customs, a blend of joyous chaos and quiet contemplation. We navigated the cultural differences with a combination of humor, patience, and a willingness to compromise. There were moments of frustration, moments of laughter, moments of quiet reflection, and even a few tears.

There was the incident with the latkes. My stepmother, determined to embrace the full Hanukkah experience, attempted to make latkes from scratch. The result was a culinary disaster of epic proportions – burnt, greasy pancakes that resembled nothing so much as small, crispy hockey pucks. The children, ever resilient, bravely consumed them nonetheless, while the adults discreetly relegated them to the compost pile.

Yet, amidst the chaos and occasional culinary catastrophes, a remarkable sense of unity emerged. We celebrated the differences, recognizing them as sources of richness and depth rather than obstacles to overcome. We learned from each other, expanding our understanding of the world and its myriad cultures.

By the time the holidays concluded, we were exhausted, but also deeply satisfied. We had created a Christmas—and a Kwanzaa, and a Hanukkah—that was uniquely our own, a kaleidoscope of traditions that reflected our own unique family tapestry. It wasn't perfect. It was messy, chaotic, and at times, utterly hilarious. But it was ours, and it was a testament to the power of love, laughter, and the ability to find harmony even in the midst of a multicultural holiday maelstrom.

And the children? They were simply thrilled. Their eyes sparkled with the magic of multiple holidays, their hearts full of the joy of giving and receiving, their minds enriched by the exposure to diverse traditions and cultural perspectives. They had witnessed firsthand the beauty of embracing differences, and that, in itself, was the most precious gift of all. It was a legacy we were painstakingly creating, one filled with laughter, love, and the occasional slightly burnt latke. And as I watched them, I knew that the multi-cultural Christmas we'd cobbled together had become more than just a holiday celebration; it was the foundation of a family, interwoven with threads of love, respect, and a profound appreciation for the tapestry of human experience. A future where our differences are celebrated was becoming a reality, not just a hopeful dream. The future's melody was already playing, a symphony composed by our laughter and love, the harmony found not in sameness, but in the beautiful diversity of our family. A family where the holiday spirit transcended tradition, creating its own unique holiday cheer, a testament to our ever-evolving multicultural Christmas legacy.

The New Year arrived, a fresh start, but the echoes of the holiday season's chaotic harmony still resonated within our blended family. The lingering scent of pine needles battled with the faint aroma of fried chicken, a testament to the culinary battles fought and won (mostly won, with a few strategic retreats). The kids, however, seemed to have fully embraced the multi-cultural maelstrom. They now seamlessly transitioned between discussing the merits of Kwanzaa's seven principles and the strategic placement of dreidels during Hanukkah. My stepmother and I exchanged amused glances, a silent acknowledgment of our shared journey through the holiday whirlwind.

This newfound ease wasn't a result of some magical holiday miracle; it was the product of hard-won compromises and a growing understanding of each other's traditions. We'd learned that the key wasn't to eliminate differences but to find ways to celebrate them. The Christmas tree, still standing proudly (albeit slightly less adorned) in the corner, became a symbol of this evolving understanding. We decided to keep it up longer, creating a sort of extended, multicultural festive season.

My mother, however, remained a staunch defender of tradition. Her attempts to subtly steer us back towards a more "conventional" Christmas were met with a mixture of amusement and gentle resistance. One afternoon, while we were attempting to assemble a rather complicated origami crane under her watchful eye (a new addition to our multicultural Christmas repertoire), she launched into a detailed critique of my stepmother's Christmas pudding.

"It lacked soul," she declared, stirring her tea with a dramatic flourish. "Too much brandy, not enough... well, everything really. Christmas pudding should be a reflection of the heart, not some fancy, over-engineered dessert."

My stepmother, ever the diplomat, responded with a calm smile. "I'll keep that in mind for next year, Mother. Perhaps we can have a pudding-making competition?"

My mother considered this suggestion, her lips pursed in thought. The idea of a pudding-making competition, a direct challenge to her culinary supremacy, was clearly intriguing.

The competition, when it finally took place, was a masterclass in controlled chaos. My mother, armed with her grandmother's recipe book and a steely determination, proceeded with military precision. My stepmother, meanwhile, approached the task with an almost scientific approach, meticulously measuring ingredients and consulting various culinary websites on her phone. The children, naturally, were enlisted as taste-testers, providing enthusiastic (though somewhat unreliable) feedback.

The results were surprisingly delightful. My mother's pudding, a rich, dark, and deeply traditional creation, was a tribute to years of culinary heritage. My stepmother's, lighter and more modern, was a testament to her innovative spirit. The judges (the children) declared it a tie, their verdict met with cheers and a surprisingly touching moment of mutual respect between the two women. The victory, however, felt less like a win and more like a mutual understanding. They had found a way to reconcile their contrasting styles, proving that even in the kitchen, a multicultural harmony could flourish.

The following months brought their own set of challenges and triumphs. Easter, for example, was celebrated with a mixture of hot cross buns, elaborate Easter egg hunts, and a surprisingly effective attempt at making matzah ball soup (a Passover dish) that didn't turn the soup into a gelatinous blob. These experiences, each unique in their own way, further reinforced the growing understanding within our family. We were learning to navigate cultural differences, not with awkward silence, but with laughter, playful teasing, and a shared appreciation for the richness of our diverse heritage.

One evening, while sitting around the fire, sharing stories and laughter, my stepmother looked at me with a thoughtful expression. "You know," she said, "I never thought I'd be celebrating Kwanzaa, Hanukkah, and Christmas all in one holiday season. But it's... surprisingly wonderful."

I smiled, feeling a warmth spread through me. "Me neither," I replied. "But it's also... surprisingly us."

The journey hadn't been easy. There were moments of friction, occasional misunderstandings, and the occasional culinary catastrophe. But we'd learned to laugh at ourselves, to celebrate our differences, and to find common ground amidst the chaos. We had created a unique family dynamic, a blend of traditions and cultures that was undeniably us. We were no longer simply blending families; we were creating something entirely new, something beautiful and uniquely our own.

This wasn't merely the merging of two families; it was the creation of a new cultural tapestry, vibrant and complex, a masterpiece woven from the threads of our diverse heritages. Our holiday celebrations were no longer a series of separate events, but a continuous, joyful narrative, a testament to the power of love and acceptance in the face of cultural differences. The children, our silent observers, were absorbing all of this, learning invaluable lessons about tolerance, understanding, and the beauty of diversity. Their future was being shaped not only by our words but by our actions, by the way we embraced our differences and celebrated the unique richness of our blended family.

The key, I realized, wasn't about erasing differences or forcing conformity. It was about creating space for everyone's traditions, embracing the unique flavors and textures of each culture, and finding harmony in the delightful cacophony of our family life. The laughter, the occasional minor conflicts, the shared meals, and the memories created during those unconventional holidays were forging a bond stronger than any single tradition. It was building a family founded on respect, understanding, and a deep appreciation for the vibrant mosaic of our multicultural identity. A family that not only survived but thrived amidst the joyous chaos of our evolving holiday celebrations. A family where the holiday spirit extended far beyond the tinsel and the twinkling lights, creating a legacy of love, acceptance, and the unique joy of a truly multicultural Christmas, Kwanzaa, and Hanukkah. And that, I knew, was a legacy worth celebrating.

The doorbell rang, a shrill, insistent chime that sliced through the post-dinner quiet. My stepmother, still humming a jaunty Christmas carol slightly off-key, glanced at me with a raised eyebrow. The kids, sprawled on the floor amidst a chaotic landscape of board games and discarded candy wrappers, barely registered the interruption. Only my mother, ever vigilant, sat bolt upright, her teacup trembling slightly in her hand.

"Who on earth could that be?" she muttered, her voice laced with a mixture of suspicion and apprehension.

I shrugged, expecting a neighbor or perhaps a late-arriving relative. The possibility of a surprise visit from my estranged Uncle Jerome never truly left my mind, but I'd learned to keep that particular anxiety at bay.

The door opened to reveal Aunt Mildred, my mother's sister, a woman whose personality could best be described as a walking, talking tornado of eccentric energy. She swept into the house like a gust of wind, a whirlwind of brightly colored scarves, jangling bracelets, and an overwhelming scent of lavender and something vaguely resembling gingerbread.

"Surprise!" she boomed, her voice echoing through the already bustling house. "I just couldn't resist! Heard you were having a multicultural extravaganza, and I simply had to partake in the festive chaos!"

My mother's face was a mixture of shock and barely concealed horror. Aunt Mildred, bless her cotton socks, possessed a unique ability to disrupt any gathering, no matter how carefully planned. She'd once single-handedly derailed a family wedding by attempting to perform a spontaneous interpretive dance during the vows.

"Mildred!" my mother exclaimed, her voice a mix of exasperation and resignation. "You didn't even call!"

"Darling, where's the fun in that?" Aunt Mildred retorted, already unpacking a massive, elaborately wrapped gift from her overflowing handbag. "Besides, I'm starving! Is there any of that... what was it... matzah ball soup left? I've always wanted to try it!"

The matzah ball soup, a surprisingly successful experiment from our Passover-Easter fusion, had become the unlikely star of our recent culinary adventures. It had brought an unexpected element of harmony to our family, a symbol of our evolving understanding. Now, however, Aunt Mildred's sudden and unexpected appearance threatened to undo all our hard-earned progress.

The kids, however, were thrilled. Aunt Mildred possessed an uncanny ability to engage children, transforming even the most mundane tasks into fantastical adventures. Within minutes, she had them involved in a game of improvised charades, their laughter echoing through the house like a joyful chorus. My stepmother, ever adaptable, joined in with surprising enthusiasm, her initial apprehension melting away under Aunt Mildred's infectious energy.

My mother, however, remained unimpressed. She watched from a distance, her lips pursed in a thin line, a silent testament to her enduring battle against festive chaos. The tension in the room was palpable, a silent clash between tradition and spontaneity, order and chaos.

Aunt Mildred's presence, though initially unwelcome, unexpectedly became a catalyst for further hilarity and misunderstanding. Her attempts to contribute to our multicultural celebration were, to put it mildly, unconventional. She insisted on adding glitter to the Kwanzaa kinara, declared that the dreidels needed a more "flamboyant" design, and attempted to incorporate her own unique brand of interpretive dance into the Christmas carols.

The ensuing chaos was glorious. The kids, utterly enchanted by Aunt Mildred's unconventional approach, were in stitches. My stepmother, ever the diplomat, tried to maintain some semblance of order, subtly redirecting Aunt Mildred's creative impulses. My mother, however, was on the verge of a nervous breakdown.

The highlight of the evening, however, was Aunt Mildred's attempt at making a Hanukkah sufganiyot, a jelly-filled doughnut. She'd decided, based on a vague memory of a cooking show she'd seen years ago, that the secret ingredient was a generous dash of lavender. The results were, to put it mildly, disastrous. The doughnuts were oddly purple, the lavender scent overpowering even Aunt Mildred's perfume, and the texture resembled something closer to a rubber ball than a delicate pastry.

The children, however, found the lavender-infused sufganiyot hilarious, their laughter filling the room. Even my mother cracked a smile, a rare and precious event that felt like a victory in itself. The lavender disaster, far from being a catastrophe, had somehow become a symbol of our family's unique blend of cultural quirks and unconventional celebrations. It was a reminder that even amidst the chaos, there was a surprising amount of love, laughter, and an undeniable sense of belonging.

As the night wore on, and Aunt Mildred eventually – albeit reluctantly – departed, a strange sense of calm settled over the house. The lingering scent of lavender and gingerbread mingled with the familiar aromas of pine needles and fried chicken, a bizarre but oddly comforting perfume of our unconventional holiday celebration.

The next morning, as we surveyed the aftermath of Aunt Mildred's visit, the house still echoing with her laughter and the faint aroma of lavender, a profound realization dawned on me. It wasn't the carefully planned traditions or the perfectly executed recipes that defined our family, but the unexpected moments, the unexpected guests, and the glorious chaos that somehow managed to bring us closer together. We were a family forged in the fires of intercultural misunderstandings and culinary mishaps, a family bound by laughter, love, and an unwavering capacity for creating unforgettable, and often hilariously chaotic, memories. And that, I knew, was something truly special. This wasn't just a holiday season; it was a testament to the power of love, acceptance, and the surprising beauty of a perfectly imperfect family. The memories we made that year, the laughter, the shared moments of near-disaster, those were the true gifts of the season. And, in the midst of the chaos, I realized we weren't just surviving – we were thriving. We were a family, a true, beautiful, and wonderfully imperfect family. And that was more precious than any perfectly executed tradition. The holiday season, with all its unconventional twists and turns, had woven itself into the very fabric of who we were, creating a tapestry of shared experiences that were as uniquely us as the fingerprints on our hands. And that, I knew, was a legacy worth cherishing.

The aftermath of Aunt Mildred's visit resembled a battlefield after a particularly festive and chaotic war. Glitter still clung to the Kwanzaa kinara like stubborn confetti, a testament to her unwavering belief in the power of sparkly embellishments. The dreidels, now adorned with what could only be described as abstract art created using felt-tip pens and glue, looked less like traditional spinning tops and more like bizarre, multi-colored mutant insects. And the lingering aroma of lavender, a scent previously associated only with Aunt Mildred's eccentric perfume, now permeated every corner of the house, clinging to the curtains, the furniture, and even the dog.

My stepmother, ever the pragmatist, took charge of the cleanup, armed with a feather duster, a vacuum cleaner, and a surprisingly cheerful demeanor. She hummed a Christmas carol, albeit a slightly different one this time, her movements as graceful and efficient as a professional cleaner in a particularly festive movie montage. The kids, energized by the lingering excitement of Aunt Mildred's visit, helped with surprising enthusiasm, their laughter punctuating the rhythmic whirring of the vacuum cleaner.

My mother, however, remained a silent observer, perched on a stool in the corner, nursing a cup of tea and observing the proceedings with a mixture of amusement and weary acceptance. She had finally surrendered to the chaos, realizing that resistance was futile. The battle against festive disorder had been lost, but in its place had sprung up a surprising sense of unity, a shared experience that had somehow brought the family closer together.

The holiday dilemmas, however, were far from over. The annual family Christmas party loomed, a gathering that always threatened to devolve into a spectacular display of dysfunctional family dynamics. This year, the challenge was compounded by the fact that we were hosting not only my mother's side of the family, steeped in traditional Christmas customs, but also my stepmother's, whose family celebrated Hanukkah with gusto.

The prospect of merging two distinctly different cultural celebrations into a single harmonious event seemed daunting, even for my ever-resourceful stepmother. The idea of blending traditional Christmas carols with Hanukkah songs, of serving both roast turkey and latkes, seemed like a recipe for disaster. My mother, naturally, was already preparing a detailed itinerary, a meticulously planned schedule designed to ensure that every tradition was observed with unwavering precision.

My stepmother, sensing the impending clash of cultures, suggested a different approach. Instead of trying to force a fusion of traditions, she proposed celebrating each holiday separately, but in a way that celebrated both cultures. She suggested a Christmas Eve dinner featuring traditional Christmas fare, followed by a Hanukkah celebration on Christmas Day, complete with menorah lighting, dreidel spinning, and a mountain of latkes, courtesy of her own family's legendary recipe.

This approach, though unconventional, proved to be surprisingly effective. My mother, initially hesitant, eventually agreed, realizing that it offered a solution that respected both cultural traditions without sacrificing the essence of the holiday spirit. The kids, delighted by the prospect of two separate celebrations, enthusiastically embraced the plan.

The Christmas Eve dinner was a resounding success. The traditional roast turkey, perfectly cooked and beautifully presented, was devoured with gusto. The Christmas carols, sung with heartfelt enthusiasm, filled the house with warmth and cheer. My mother, beaming with pride, watched as her family happily engaged in the familiar rituals of the holiday season.

Christmas Day dawned bright and cheerful, bringing with it the promise of a different kind of celebration. This time, the focus shifted to Hanukkah. My stepmother's family, a boisterous and energetic bunch, arrived bearing gifts and overflowing platters of latkes. The menorah was lit, its flickering flames casting a warm glow on the faces of the assembled family.

The dreidels spun, their whirring a playful counterpoint to the laughter and chatter that filled the room. The children, thoroughly engaged in the festive spirit, gleefully collected their winnings, their faces alight with excitement. My mother, initially skeptical, found herself drawn into the spirit of the celebration, marveling at the warmth and joy that emanated from my stepmother's family.

The merging of the two families, two cultures, two distinct holiday traditions, had not been a seamless process. There had been moments of tension, of awkward silences, of cultural misunderstandings. But amidst the chaos and the occasional clash, a new sense of togetherness had emerged. We weren't just celebrating two different holidays; we were celebrating the unique tapestry of our family, a vibrant blend of cultures, traditions, and personalities.

Even Aunt Mildred's unexpected appearance, a whirlwind of lavender-scented chaos, had somehow contributed to the overall festive harmony. Her eccentric attempts to blend Hanukkah and Christmas traditions, however bizarre, had added an element of unexpected hilarity and a surprising sense of unity.

The holiday season, with its myriad challenges and unexpected twists, had tested our family's resilience, its ability to adapt, to overcome differences, and to find joy amidst the chaos. And in the end, we had not only survived but thrived. We had created memories that would be cherished for years to come, memories that were uniquely ours, reflecting our diverse family, our individual quirks, and the surprising beauty of our unconventional celebrations.

The lingering aroma of lavender, a quirky reminder of Aunt Mildred's visit, mingled with the scent of pine needles, the taste of turkey, and the savory goodness of latkes. It was a unique perfume, a blend of traditions and cultures, a testament to the enduring power of family, love, and the ability to find harmony, even amidst the most festive of chaos. This wasn't just a holiday season; it was a testament to the strength and resilience of a family that had learned to embrace its differences, celebrate its uniqueness, and find joy in the unpredictable journey of life. And as we looked forward to the new year, we carried with us the laughter, the love, and the wonderfully imperfect memories of our uniquely blended holiday celebration. It was a reminder that family wasn't about perfect traditions or flawless executions, but about shared moments, laughter, and the ability to find joy in the unpredictable and beautifully messy tapestry of life.

The New Year's Eve party, a smaller, more intimate affair compared to the Christmas extravaganza, felt like a quiet exhale after a whirlwind holiday season. The lingering scent of latkes and pine needles had been replaced by the crisp, clean air of a new beginning. My mother, surprisingly, had opted for a simple, elegant black dress, a far cry from her usual festive attire. Even her hair, usually meticulously styled, was loosely pulled back, hinting at a relaxed sense of contentment. My stepmother, equally radiant, wore a sleek, emerald green gown that shimmered subtly under the soft lighting. They stood together, a testament to their unlikely but undeniable bond, a visual representation of the festive harmony they had managed to forge.

The children, exhausted but happy, were tucked away in bed, their dreams likely filled with visions of spinning dreidels and mountains of latkes. The adults, however, were still buzzing with the energy of the past few weeks, their conversations a lively mix of reminiscences, laughter, and shared stories. My stepmother's family, having bid us farewell earlier in the evening, left behind a trail of warm wishes and a lingering sense of camaraderie.

My mother, leaning back in her chair, sipped her champagne, a gentle smile playing on her lips. "You know," she began, her voice soft and contemplative, "I never thought I'd see the day when I'd be comfortable celebrating Hanukkah." Her admission surprised me, but the genuine affection in her tone made it clear that she meant every word. There was a sense of wonder in her voice, a recognition of the unexpected joys that had emerged from embracing a different culture.

My stepmother chuckled, her eyes sparkling with mirth. "And I never thought I'd be able to make your mother's traditional Christmas pudding without setting off the smoke alarm," she retorted, drawing laughter from everyone present. Her lightheartedness defused any potential awkwardness, highlighting the humor in their shared journey. The unexpected alliances, the blending of traditions, the very essence of their unconventional family, had become a source of joy and shared experience.

The conversation flowed easily, weaving between anecdotes from the past few weeks, from the near-disaster of Aunt Mildred's glitter-bomb attack to the surprisingly successful merging of Christmas and Hanukkah traditions. We recounted the children's hilarious reactions to the unusual combination of cultural celebrations, their gleeful participation in both festive rituals, and their unwavering enthusiasm for the seemingly endless supply of sweets. The anecdotes served as a reminder of the shared experiences, the laughter, and the love that had bound us together during this special time of year.

The evening gradually wound down, the laughter softening into quiet conversation. The air was filled with a sense of quiet contentment, a peaceful acknowledgment of the unexpected joy that had bloomed from the unlikely fusion of two distinctly different cultures. The year had begun with apprehension, uncertainty, and the looming specter of potential holiday chaos, yet it had culminated in a surprising sense of unity, understanding, and shared happiness.

As the clock chimed midnight, ushering in the New Year, we raised our glasses in a toast to the year gone by, a year that had brought with it its fair share of challenges but also its abundance of unexpected blessings. We toasted to the resilience of our unconventional family, its ability to adapt, to overcome differences, and to find joy amidst the most festive chaos. We toasted to the unexpected friendships that had blossomed, the cultural barriers that had been broken down, and the love that had strengthened and bound us all together.

The following morning dawned bright and clear, promising a new year filled with possibilities. The house, quiet and peaceful, was a stark contrast to the festive whirlwind of the previous weeks. The lingering scents of holiday cheer – the pine needles, the cinnamon, the faint trace of Aunt Mildred's lavender perfume – served as a sweet reminder of the laughter, love, and unforgettable moments that had shaped our holiday season.

The cleanup, undertaken with a shared sense of camaraderie, felt less like a chore and more like a final act of togetherness. We recounted funny anecdotes from the past few weeks, sharing memories that made us laugh until our stomachs ached. The act of putting the house back in order mirrored the subtle yet profound shift in our family dynamic. The chaos had subsided, replaced by a quiet sense of harmony, a testament to our ability to adapt, embrace differences, and find joy in the beautifully messy tapestry of life.

As the new year unfolded, we carried with us the lessons learned during the holiday season. We had learned to embrace the unconventional, to laugh in the face of adversity, and to find unity amidst the chaos. We had discovered that family wasn't defined by shared bloodlines or matching traditions, but by shared experiences, mutual respect, and an unwavering commitment to one another.

The differences that had initially threatened to divide us had, in fact, become the very foundation of our unique and surprisingly harmonious family. The blending of Christmas and Hanukkah traditions had not only created a richer, more meaningful celebration but had also laid bare the universality of love, joy, and the human need for connection. We had found common ground not in the superficial similarities of our cultures but in the fundamental values that underpinned both of our traditions.

The once-daunting task of bridging two vastly different cultures had, unexpectedly, forged a new level of understanding and appreciation between my mother and stepmother. Their initial hesitancy had given way to a mutual respect, a recognition of each other's unique strengths, and an enduring commitment to creating a loving and supportive family environment for their children.

The children, oblivious to the initial complexities of blending two very different cultural backgrounds, had effortlessly embraced the unique mix of traditions. They had found joy in the simple act of sharing experiences, in the laughter and warmth of family gatherings, and in the abundance of festive treats. Their innocent enthusiasm had, in a way, served as a beacon, guiding the adults towards a more harmonious and inclusive approach to celebrating their holiday traditions.

This new sense of family harmony wasn't merely a fleeting holiday phenomenon, but a profound transformation that resonated far beyond the festive season. It served as a foundation for a stronger, more united family, one that embraced its diversity and drew strength from its shared experiences. The memories of laughter, the warmth of family, and the surprising sense of harmony would remain not just as cherished recollections of a particular holiday season, but as a testament to their enduring resilience, their adaptability, and their capacity to find joy in the beautifully imperfect and wonderfully unconventional tapestry of their family life. The New Year, bright with promise, held the potential for more adventures, more laughter, and more unconventional celebrations, all woven into the rich tapestry of their uniquely beautiful and forever evolving family.

Chapter 8: Growing Together

The tranquility of the new year didn't last long. The quiet harmony, the carefully constructed peace, began to unravel as the children, our delightfully chaotic brood, entered a new phase of their lives. It wasn't a sudden explosion, more of a slow, creeping realization that the idyllic family portrait we'd painstakingly crafted was starting to crack at the edges. The cracks, initially hairline fissures, were caused by the ever-shifting tectonic plates of adolescence.

My eldest, Leah, a bright, fiercely independent teenager, was grappling with the complexities of high school. Her world, once filled with the uncomplicated joys of building snow forts and devouring mountains of latkes, was now a complicated tapestry of social hierarchies, academic pressures, and the bewildering landscape of first crushes. The transition was particularly challenging because she was navigating this new terrain against the backdrop of our unconventional family. While she loved both her mothers, there were moments when she felt the weight of being the "other" – the child in the interracial, blended family, constantly explaining, justifying, and navigating the sometimes-subtle, sometimes-not-so-subtle stares and whispers.

Then there was David, my younger son, who was navigating the choppy waters of pre-teen angst. His quiet, introspective nature, once a source of amusement, was now tinged with a brooding intensity that I wasn't quite sure how to handle. He was grappling with the usual pre-teen anxieties – fitting in, finding his place, the overwhelming desire to be accepted, but his concerns also stemmed from the same sources as Leah's: navigating his place in a family that wasn't exactly like the other families in school.

The differences between my wife and my mother, once a source of amusing anecdotes, now sometimes felt like fault lines that could erupt without warning. My mother, still holding firm to many of her traditional views, found some of Leah's fashion choices and David's emerging cynicism particularly difficult to comprehend. My wife, on the other hand, was often more tolerant, seeing their behaviors as typical teenage manifestations. These differences in approach, while not inherently negative, frequently led to friction, subtle disagreements, and the occasional, thinly veiled eye roll exchanged between the two women. The constant negotiation of parenting styles became a source of stress, threatening to erode the fragile peace that had been established over the holidays.

One evening, during a particularly fraught dinner conversation – fueled by Leah's refusal to participate in family game night and David's sullen silence – the tension boiled over. My mother, bless her heart, launched into a monologue about the importance of family values and respecting elders, her voice tinged with a familiar undercurrent of frustration. My wife, sensing her mother-in-law was about to cross a line, gently but firmly interjected, suggesting we might all benefit from some personal space. The ensuing silence was thick with unspoken words, the unspoken anxieties of two very different women trying to navigate the turbulent waters of modern family dynamics.

This incident forced me to confront a harsh reality. The seemingly harmonious family dynamic we had cultivated wasn't just a matter of managing cultural differences anymore; it involved navigating the complexities of raising teenagers in a blended, interracial family. The challenges weren't just about bridging cultural divides; they were about finding common ground in parenting styles, communicating effectively through generational differences, and managing the inevitable friction that arose from the contrasting perspectives of my mother and my wife.

The situation prompted several family meetings, conversations that were often more akin to delicately choreographed dance routines than straightforward discussions. We had to acknowledge the elephant in the room: our differences weren't going away, but we could choose how we handled them. We tried to establish clear communication channels, encourage empathy, and foster a more inclusive environment where each family member felt heard and respected. It wasn't easy, and there were plenty of setbacks.

Leah started attending therapy, a decision that brought a wave of relief and a tinge of guilt. It felt like an admission of failure, a recognition that I wasn't equipped to handle the complexities of her emotional landscape. But therapy provided her with a safe space to explore her feelings, navigate her identity, and cope with the unique challenges of her interracial, blended family life. It also helped her articulate her needs to us in a healthier way.

David, in his quieter way, started engaging in activities he enjoyed, joining a robotics club and finding a sense of belonging amongst his peers. His newfound passion redirected some of his energy, giving him an outlet for his anxieties and a newfound sense of self-confidence. His quiet contentment became a balm, smoothing out some of the rough edges in the family dynamic.

My wife and mother, realizing the limitations of their individual approaches, began to appreciate each other's strengths. They started seeking compromises, actively listening to each other's concerns, and finding common ground in their shared love for the children. They weren't suddenly best friends, but there was a growing mutual respect, a recognition that they were both striving towards the same goal: creating a loving, supportive home for our children.

This process was slow, painstaking, and at times, profoundly frustrating. There were arguments, misunderstandings, and moments when I questioned whether we were even capable of navigating this turbulent sea. But there were also moments of profound connection, shared laughter, and a quiet appreciation for the strength and resilience of our unconventional family. We learned that family harmony wasn't a destination, but an ongoing journey, a constant negotiation, and an unwavering commitment to understanding and supporting each other.

The challenges continued, of course. The teenage years are rarely calm waters. But we were learning, adapting, and growing together. We were learning to embrace the imperfections, the arguments, and the occasional chaotic outburst as part of the beautiful, messy tapestry of family life. We found strength in our shared experiences, in the unique bond we'd forged through laughter and tears, through celebrations and arguments, through cultural clashes and shared joys.

What we discovered was that the real magic wasn't in seamlessly blending two different cultures, but in acknowledging the differences, respecting individual perspectives, and finding joy in the beautiful chaos of our imperfectly perfect, wonderfully unconventional family. It was a testament to the enduring power of love, resilience, and the unwavering commitment to creating a loving home where everyone felt valued, accepted, and loved, regardless of their background, their opinions, or their current stage of adolescent turmoil. The new challenges, though daunting, ultimately served to strengthen the bonds that held us together. They forged a deeper understanding, not just between my wife and my mother, but within the family as a whole. We were learning, growing, and discovering the surprising joy of facing life's challenges together, as a family, in all our imperfectly perfect glory.

The following summer brought a whirlwind of activity. Leah, surprisingly, landed a coveted internship at a local fashion magazine, a testament to her burgeoning talent and relentless drive. The internship, however, meant long hours, early mornings, and a significant shift in her schedule. This threw our carefully constructed family routines into disarray, causing a fresh wave of adjustments and compromises. My mother, ever the pragmatist, saw it as an opportunity for Leah to learn responsibility and gain valuable experience; my wife, however, worried about the impact on Leah's already demanding academic workload. The ensuing discussions were less about the internship itself and more about the fundamental differences in their parenting philosophies – a familiar dance we'd grown accustomed to.

David, meanwhile, was thriving in his robotics club. His quiet intensity found an outlet, his quiet anxieties a channel of expression. He was building robots, winning competitions, and, astonishingly, making friends. His newfound confidence seeped into other aspects of his life, softening his edges, improving his mood, and even improving his relationship with his sister. It was amazing to witness. This newfound passion also led to some unexpected benefits, one of which was a much-needed truce between my mother and wife. My mother, initially hesitant about David's obsession with technology ("Too much screen time!" was her battle cry), became impressed by his ingenuity and determination, even volunteering to help him with a particularly intricate project involving soldering and circuit boards. This small act of shared activity, this unlikely alliance over shared effort and success, fostered a newfound level of understanding between the two women. It was a small crack in the wall, a thin beam of light in the formerly shadowy corridors of our family dynamics.

My wife and I, seeing the positive impact of these individual developments, began to consciously prioritize "family time," though this sometimes turned out to be more ambitious than realistic. Our family dinners, once a battleground of adolescent angst and simmering tensions, were now infused with more laughter, shared stories, and a genuine sense of connection. We started incorporating little traditions, making a point of watching a favorite movie together on Saturday nights, going for family walks in the park on Sundays, and cooking dinner together, despite the ensuing kitchen chaos. These seemingly small gestures had an enormous impact on the overall atmosphere at home. The shared experiences—even the messy ones—helped reinforce our bonds, strengthening the ties that held us together.

One particular evening, while attempting to build a disastrously lopsided gingerbread house, Leah burst into tears, overwhelmed by a combination of academic pressure, the stress of her internship, and the general complexities of being a teenager. It wasn't a dramatic, attention-seeking meltdown; it was a quiet, heart-wrenching collapse, a silent surrender to the weight of it all. My mother, to our surprise, was the first to react. She gently wrapped her arm around Leah, offering words of comfort and support, a gesture that spoke volumes about the slow but steady shift in their relationship. My wife joined them, offering a cup of tea and a listening ear. The scene, utterly unexpected, felt momentous, marking the turning point in their relationship; that silent moment of unity was a potent testament to their growing bond, a silent affirmation of their shared commitment to our unconventional family.

These shared moments, both big and small, gradually reshaped our family dynamic. We learned to celebrate each other's successes, offering words of encouragement during times of struggle, and providing a constant flow of unwavering support. The challenges remained – teenagers are notoriously unpredictable creatures, and intergenerational misunderstandings are a fact of life – but our approach to those challenges had changed. We learned the value of active listening, of acknowledging each other's feelings, and of finding ways to navigate our differences without sacrificing our mutual respect.

The ongoing therapy sessions for Leah proved invaluable. Not only did they help her cope with the pressures of her teenage years, but they also provided a safe space for her to explore her identity in the context of our unique family dynamic. She learned to articulate her feelings, express her needs, and advocate for herself in a healthy and productive manner. The improvement was evident; her mood lightened, her confidence grew, and her interactions with both her mothers became more open and honest.

David's passion for robotics also helped him forge stronger relationships outside the family. He became more outgoing, making genuine connections with his peers, and developing friendships that enriched his life. He even began to mentor younger children in the robotics club, showcasing his developing leadership skills and quiet selflessness. His blossoming confidence further eased the tension within the family, providing a sense of collective pride and accomplishment.

My mother and wife, while never becoming best friends, developed a grudging respect for each other's strengths. They found common ground in their shared love for their grandchildren and a mutual understanding of the challenges of raising teenagers. There were still moments of disagreement, but those disagreements were less frequent, less volatile, and more easily resolved. They began communicating more effectively, showing a willingness to compromise and a genuine desire to understand each other's perspectives. This new dynamic extended beyond their own relationship; their improved communication positively impacted the rest of the family.

Our unconventional family continued to face its share of challenges. There were still moments of friction, misunderstandings, and the occasional adolescent outburst. But these moments became less significant, less disruptive, and easier to navigate. We learned to accept our imperfections, to laugh at our mistakes, and to find strength in our shared experiences. We embraced the messiness of family life, understanding that it was part of the beautiful, chaotic tapestry of our unconventional family.

The journey wasn't always easy. It required patience, understanding, and a willingness to adapt and evolve. But the rewards were immeasurable. We built a stronger, more resilient family unit, bound together by a shared commitment to support and understanding, a testament to the enduring power of love, resilience, and the unwavering determination to create a loving and supportive home for our children. And through it all, we discovered that the real magic wasn't in avoiding conflict, but in facing it together, in learning from our mistakes, and in finding joy in the beautifully imperfect, wonderfully unconventional family that we had become.

Leah's angst wasn't confined to the occasional tearful gingerbread house incident. It manifested in a thousand subtle ways: slammed doors, cryptic texts, earbuds permanently affixed to her ears, a general air of simmering discontent that permeated the house like a particularly pungent cheese. One minute she'd be passionately debating the merits of vintage denim jackets with my mother, the next she'd be barricading herself in her room, emerging only to snatch a suspiciously large bag of chips before retreating back to her fortress of teenage solitude.

David, bless his heart, initially attempted to decipher the enigma that was his sister. He'd leave her carefully crafted notes filled with dad jokes and robotic puns, only to find them crumpled on her desk, unread and unappreciated. His attempts at sibling bonding usually ended with him retreating to his workshop, muttering about "the illogical emotional programming of adolescents." My mother, ever the observer, found this a source of amusement, often remarking that David's attempts at emotional engagement were as clunky and predictable as his early robotics projects.

My wife and I, however, found ourselves increasingly caught in the crossfire. We'd try to reason with Leah, to understand the root of her frustration, only to be met with monosyllabic answers and the aforementioned slammed doors. My wife, ever the nurturer, would attempt to engage her in heart-to-heart talks, while I, resorting to my more pragmatic approach, would try to offer logical solutions, which were often met with eye-rolls that could curdle milk.

One particularly chaotic morning, Leah's frustration boiled over during a particularly stressful breakfast. She'd overslept, missed the bus, and was facing the prospect of being late for a crucial fashion shoot. The ensuing chaos involved a frantic search for missing shoes, a near-miss with a scalding cup of coffee, and a series of exasperated sighs that echoed throughout the house. My mother, ever-present in the background, observed the scene with a mixture of amusement and concern, offering helpful (and largely ignored) suggestions from her perch on the kitchen counter.

"Perhaps if you laid out your clothes the night before," she suggested, in the tone of someone who'd witnessed this same scenario play out countless times.

Leah, in response, simply threw a pair of crumpled jeans onto the table, eliciting a perfectly-timed "I told you so" from my mother. My wife, sensing the growing tension, intervened, attempting to calm Leah down and get her to school on time.

The whole episode, though stressful, proved to be a turning point. Later that day, after Leah returned from a successful shoot, she surprisingly thanked my wife for her help that morning. Then, even more surprisingly, she apologized for her behavior. This small act of acknowledgement opened up a dialogue, a rare glimpse into the whirlwind of emotions that were swirling within her.

It turned out that much of Leah's anxiety stemmed not just from the pressures of her internship and school, but also from a growing awareness of her identity in our diverse family. She felt the weight of navigating the different expectations and cultural nuances associated with her heritage, her mother's heritage, and the blended tapestry of our lives. The therapy sessions she'd been attending were helping her to articulate these feelings, and she felt empowered to share them with us.

This opened up a crucial opportunity for us to foster more meaningful conversations. We began to actively listen to Leah, asking her open-ended questions, creating a space where she felt safe to express her doubts and fears without judgment. We were careful not to dismiss her concerns as mere teenage angst. Instead, we validated her feelings, reminding her that it was okay to feel overwhelmed, to feel confused, and to seek clarity in a world that often felt chaotic.

David, initially hesitant to participate in these conversations, gradually found himself drawn into the emotional orbit of his sister's journey of self-discovery. He surprised us all by offering his own insights, drawing parallels between the complexity of human relationships and the intricate workings of his robots. He pointed out that even the most sophisticated machines require calibration and adjustments, just as humans require understanding and patience.

His observation, while seemingly simple, resonated deeply with everyone. It became a powerful metaphor for our family dynamic, a reminder that growth and understanding require constant adjustments, a willingness to embrace imperfection and to learn from our mistakes.

My mother, who previously approached Leah's teenage angst with a blend of bemusement and exasperation, began to show a newfound empathy. She shared stories of her own teenage years, revealing a side of her personality we hadn't known before. It was during one of these sharing sessions that I discovered the remarkable resilience of my own mother, her strength forged in the fires of her youth. She admitted that she was still learning to navigate her relationship with her daughter and daughter-in-law, but her willingness to share her vulnerabilities and her desire to improve created a powerful connection.

The conversations were not always easy. There were moments of tension, of misunderstandings, of the occasional eruption of teenage frustration. But the difference was that we now had a framework for navigating these challenges. We were actively listening, actively learning, actively growing together. We celebrated small victories, acknowledging progress even when faced with setbacks.

The summer that followed was a testament to the progress we'd made. Leah thrived in her internship, continuing to impress her colleagues and solidifying her passion for fashion. Her newfound confidence was evident in every aspect of her life, from the way she carried herself to her interactions with her peers. David, ever the steadfast presence, continued to shine in his robotics club, mentoring younger students and nurturing his passion for technology.

My mother and wife, though still vastly different, had found a common ground in their shared love for their children and their grandchildren. They still had their moments of disagreement, but these disagreements were less frequent, less volatile, and more easily resolved. They were learning to appreciate each other's strengths and perspectives, a testament to their growing maturity and their shared commitment to our unconventional family.

Our family dinners continued to evolve, becoming less of a battleground and more of a celebration of our shared experiences. We laughed together, we cried together, we navigated the complexities of life together. The occasional slammed door or teenage sigh still occurred, but these moments no longer felt so disruptive, so isolating. We'd found a rhythm, a harmony that allowed for individual expression while maintaining the strength of our collective bond.

We realized that the journey of raising teenagers, particularly within an unconventional family dynamic, wasn't about avoiding conflict or achieving perfect harmony. It was about facing challenges head-on, about embracing imperfection, and about finding strength in our shared humanity. It was about learning to laugh at our mistakes and to celebrate the beautiful, chaotic tapestry of our unconventional, loving family. And in the end, that's what truly mattered. The messy, imperfect, wonderfully unconventional love that bound us together.

Our first family vacation as a blended, multi-racial unit was, shall we say, an experience. We chose a charming, if slightly dilapidated, beach house in the Outer Banks, figuring the rustic charm would outweigh any potential plumbing disasters. We were wrong. On the very first night, the showerhead decided to stage a dramatic rebellion, spraying water in every direction except the one intended. Leah, ever the pragmatist, documented the entire event on her phone, creating a slow-motion video that became an instant family meme. My mother, naturally, found the whole thing hilarious, declaring it "a true testament to the joys of affordable vacation rentals." My wife, less amused, was more concerned about the potential for mold. David, ever the engineer at heart, spent the next hour dissecting the showerhead, attempting to diagnose the problem with the same focused intensity he reserved for his robots.

The next day brought a series of misadventures worthy of a sitcom. We attempted to build a sandcastle, a project that quickly devolved into a sand-throwing war, resulting in several very sandy bathing suits and one rather upset sandpiper. My mother, in her enthusiasm, attempted to teach Leah and her sister how to surf, a venture that involved more tumbles and laughter than actual surfing. David, proving that his skills extended beyond robotics, managed to assemble a makeshift boogie board out of driftwood and duct tape, an achievement that received far more applause than my mother's surfing instruction.

The highlight (or lowlight, depending on your perspective) was our attempt at a family seafood feast. My wife, convinced that freshly caught seafood was a must, insisted that we take a fishing trip. The trip, led by a weathered, salty captain named "Salty" (naturally), involved more seasickness than actual fish-catching. My mother, who proclaimed herself a seasoned angler despite having only ever fished for compliments, ended up with a tangle of seaweed and a sunburn. Leah documented the event with alarming accuracy, which ended up on her Instagram with the caption, "Family Vacation: Seasick, sunburnt, and still no dinner."

David, to everyone's surprise, emerged as the unlikely hero, managing to reel in a surprisingly large flounder. His triumph was short-lived, however, as the flounder, upon being released from the hook, performed a miraculous escape, leaping directly into my mother's open picnic basket. The ensuing chaos involved a lot of screaming, a flurry of wildly flailing arms, and a frantic attempt to salvage the remaining contents of the picnic basket (which included a rather traumatized cheese and pickle sandwich). Even Salty cracked a rare smile, shaking his head and muttering, "I've seen a lot in my years, but nothing quite like that."

Dinner that night was decidedly less adventurous, consisting of frozen pizza and an intense discussion about the merits of different types of cheese. It was during this relatively calm evening that we began to truly appreciate the strange mix of chaos and connection that our family was creating.

The following days brought a more relaxed pace. We explored the local beaches, built bonfires, played endless games of frisbee, and shared stories that illuminated the unique cultural threads woven throughout our unconventional family. We spoke of our histories, of the sacrifices our ancestors made, of the journeys we'd each embarked upon, and of the challenges we continued to face as a multi-racial, multi-cultural family.

Leah, having had space and time to process the events of the previous days, reflected on the challenges of our family dynamics. She confessed that growing up in a diverse and blended family wasn't always easy, that there were moments where she felt the sting of other people's misconceptions. Yet, she also spoke about the richness and beauty of her identity, of the strength and love that radiated from this unusually assorted family unit.

Her perspective shifted significantly. She started to appreciate the quirks and eccentricities of her extended family members, seeing the humor in situations that previously seemed frustrating or just plain irritating. She even managed to coax David into creating a "Family Vacation Disaster" video montage, which included clips of the aforementioned showerhead incident, the sandcastle debacle, and, of course, the flounder's escape. The video received hundreds of likes and comments, proof that our family's unique brand of chaos resonated with others.

My mother, too, underwent a quiet transformation. The constant jokes and playful ribbing she directed towards my wife took on a softer tone, laced with a new appreciation of the woman who had brought such vibrancy and love into her son's life. She started to actively participate in conversations surrounding racial dynamics, admitting to past misunderstandings and a willingness to learn and grow. The previously rigid walls between them began to crumble, replaced by genuine curiosity and respect.

My wife, ever the peacemaker, found herself navigating the delicate balance between maintaining her own identity and embracing the complexities of her new family. She began to appreciate the value of tradition and culture, even trying her hand at some of my mother's traditional recipes. It wasn't always pretty, but it was honest and heartfelt. Her patience and understanding began to permeate the family, smoothing out rough edges and bridging cultural divides.

Even David, our resident robotic engineer, showed remarkable emotional growth. While he didn't necessarily express his feelings with the same effusiveness as his sister, his actions spoke volumes. He spent more time with his younger siblings, playing games and sharing his knowledge of robots and science. His interactions with my mother became more relaxed and affectionate.

The Outer Banks vacation didn't magically erase our family's differences or solve all our problems. However, it acted as a powerful catalyst for growth, forcing us to confront our fears, misunderstandings, and preconceptions. The shared experiences, both comical and challenging, created stronger bonds and fostered empathy. It was amidst the chaos of a dilapidated beach house, the unpredictability of the sea, and a rogue flounder that we truly began to grow together. We learned to laugh at the absurdity of it all, to appreciate the resilience and humor that emerged from adversity, and to cherish the messy, unconventional love that bound us together. We realized that true togetherness wasn't about avoiding conflict, but about facing it together, laughing through it all, and finding strength in our shared imperfections. And that, ultimately, was the greatest treasure of our family vacation. The following years brought more trips, more laughter, more challenges, but always with the unspoken understanding that even the most chaotic family adventures could strengthen the bonds of an unconventional but loving family.

The years following our Outer Banks escapade weren't exactly a smooth sail, but they certainly weren't devoid of laughter. We learned, the hard way, that building a blended family is akin to assembling a particularly complex piece of IKEA furniture – lots of pieces, cryptic instructions, and a high probability of ending up with extra parts you have no idea what to do with. Take, for instance, the Thanksgiving incident of 2000.

My mother, bless her heart, decided to make her legendary sweet potato pie, a recipe passed down through generations and guarded with the same fervor she reserved for her antique porcelain doll collection. Leah, ever the culinary adventurer, decided to "improve" the recipe by adding a dash of cardamom and a sprinkle of ginger. The result? A culinary catastrophe of epic proportions. The pie, instead of the usual golden brown, emerged from the oven looking more like a volcanic eruption. The smell, let's just say, was… pungent. My mother's face was a mixture of horror and disbelief. Leah, initially mortified, burst into laughter, a contagious sound that quickly spread throughout the room. Even my usually stoic wife cracked a smile, muttering something about a "spiced sweet potato lava cake." David, ever the problem-solver, suggested we just use the pie as a centerpiece, a darkly humorous reminder of our family's unconventional approach to culinary traditions. My mother eventually forgave Leah, and we all agreed to stick to the traditional recipe in the future. However, the "Spiced Sweet Potato Lava Cake" incident became a running family joke.

Christmases were a symphony of clashing cultures and comedic mishaps. One year, my mother insisted on a traditional Southern Christmas dinner with all the fixings, while my wife's family contributed a selection of Scandinavian delicacies that involved a surprising amount of herring. The combination, while initially jarring, created a strangely fascinating culinary fusion, proving that even the most unexpected pairings could result in a surprisingly delicious outcome. Another year, Leah, determined to assert her own identity within the family dynamic, decided to gift my mother a handmade ceramic sculpture of a rather abstract depiction of a bald eagle. My mother, bless her heart, loved it. David, after some awkward minutes of analysis and a lot of quiet contemplation, called it "modern art". My wife gracefully complimented the unique design, leaving everyone guessing whether she was telling the truth or just trying to keep the peace.

The family disagreements were never truly resolved, they just evolved. My mother's initial apprehension toward my wife's modern ways gradually transformed into grudging respect, sometimes even admiration. She started to appreciate my wife's easy-going nature and her ability to handle the chaos of our multi-cultural family with humor and grace. Similarly, my wife started to understand and appreciate the significance of my mother's traditions. It wasn't a seamless transition, it was a slow, bumpy ride punctuated by moments of friction, laughter, and gradual understanding. They began to bond over shared interests, surprisingly finding common ground in their love for gardening and the obsession with vintage television shows.

Leah, having reached her teenage years, found herself navigating the complex waters of identity and belonging. While initially struggling with feelings of displacement and confusion, she eventually embraced her multi-racial heritage, proudly showcasing the unique blend of cultures that shaped her identity. She transformed her initial confusion into a powerful force, expressing her experience through art and writing. Her artistic endeavors, reflecting the complex dynamics of our blended family, became a beautiful and often humorous testament to her resilience and her ability to find beauty and humor in unexpected places.

David, who had always been more comfortable with logical equations than emotional expressions, showed a surprising growth in his emotional intelligence. His interactions with his siblings and extended family became warmer and more spontaneous. He even started baking (albeit with his characteristic precision and adherence to strict measurements), creating wonderfully delicious cakes and cookies.

Maintaining harmony wasn't about eliminating conflict, but about finding ways to navigate it, to laugh at the absurdities, and to appreciate the uniqueness of our family. It was about appreciating the messy, hilarious, and unconventional nature of our diverse family. It was about learning to cherish the moments of shared joy, recognizing the value of our individuality, and understanding that genuine togetherness wasn't about uniformity, but about celebrating our differences while upholding the love and respect that bound us together.

We discovered that family isn't a perfect picture; it's a mosaic, a blend of colors and textures, sometimes clashing, sometimes harmonizing, but ultimately forming a stunning and unique masterpiece. It required constant effort, compromise, and an unwavering commitment to understanding and forgiveness. The journey wasn't always easy, filled as it was with a multitude of challenges and disagreements, but the laughter, the shared experiences, and the bonds of love far outweighed the difficulties. We learned to laugh at our mistakes, to embrace the chaos, and to recognize the beauty in the imperfections that made our family so uniquely ours.

Our family vacations became legendary—a tapestry of hilarious mishaps, unexpected adventures, and heartwarming moments of connection. A trip to Disney World resulted in a near-riot when my mother attempted to cut the line for the Space Mountain ride, while a weekend camping trip ended with a surprise visit from a family of raccoons who helped themselves to our marshmallows. Every gathering was a unique performance, a comedy show unfolding in real-time, with every member playing their part in this unique family saga.

The key to our success, if you could even call it that, was a willingness to laugh at ourselves. We embraced the absurdity of our situation, found humor in our differences, and learned to cherish the unique blend of personalities that made our family so vibrant and entertaining. It was a testament to the enduring power of love and laughter in the face of adversity, a demonstration of how embracing our differences could forge stronger bonds and create a family that was truly stronger together. The love wasn't always perfect, it was messy, chaotic, and filled with laughter – but it was ours. And that, in the end, was everything.

Chapter 9: A Legacy of Love

Leah, blossoming into a young woman, surprised us all. Her teenage years, initially marked by a quiet rebellion fueled by a sense of being somewhere between two worlds, morphed into a vibrant embrace of her dual heritage. The initial awkwardness she felt around her extended families – the hushed tones, the sideways glances, the unspoken questions – eventually gave way to a confident stride. She became a cultural ambassador of sorts, effortlessly bridging the gap between her mother's refined Scandinavian sensibilities and her father's soulful Southern charm. Her art became a powerful expression of this bridge, a vibrant tapestry weaving together seemingly disparate threads. Her paintings weren't just pretty pictures; they were narratives, stories painted in bold strokes and delicate washes, depicting the joys and challenges of growing up in a family as uniquely blended as ours. One particularly striking piece, titled "Sweet Potato Lava Cake," depicted a surreal landscape where volcanoes erupted with spiced sweet potato filling, alongside tranquil Scandinavian fjords dotted with gingerbread houses. It was both humorous and poignant, a visual representation of the often chaotic, yet deeply loving, dynamics of our family life.

Her college years were a whirlwind of creative exploration. She chose a liberal arts college known for its vibrant arts program and its commitment to diversity. There, surrounded by a kaleidoscope of cultures and perspectives, she flourished. She threw herself into her studies, excelling in art history and creative writing, her work increasingly drawing upon her personal experiences, often poking fun at the cultural clashes that shaped her childhood. One of her short stories, "Herring and Grits," became a campus sensation, a hilarious tale about a Thanksgiving dinner that somehow managed to combine both Southern comfort food and traditional Scandinavian fare – a culinary experiment that mirrored the complexities of her own family dynamic. Her work gained recognition, leading to her acceptance into a prestigious postgraduate program, further cementing her passion for artistic expression.

David, ever the pragmatist, took a different path. While he shared Leah's appreciation for the unique family tapestry they were woven into, he expressed it through a different lens. He became a software engineer, a master of algorithms and code. His logic-driven mind, once confined to the realm of mathematics, found a new outlet in the world of technology. He developed a remarkable ability to use technology to connect people, creating software solutions that fostered communication and collaboration. His creations, while seemingly far removed from Leah's artistic expressions, shared a common thread: they both helped bridge divides, fostering understanding and connection.

His ability to problem-solve, honed over years of mediating family disputes and navigating cultural misunderstandings, made him invaluable in his profession. He excelled at his work, demonstrating an innate ability to find innovative solutions to complex challenges. His dedication to his work wasn't merely about achieving professional success; it was about using his skills to make a positive impact on the world, a quiet reflection of the values instilled in him by his parents. He found great satisfaction in using technology to connect individuals, creating platforms that facilitated communication and understanding across cultures and backgrounds.

He surprised us all, however, by joining a community theater group. He discovered a hidden talent for acting, his naturally reserved demeanor surprisingly well-suited to comedic roles. He would often playfully incorporate elements of his family life into his performances, weaving in anecdotes about his mother's sweet potato pie escapades and his father's attempts at Scandinavian cooking into his skits. The blend of his serious demeanor and the humorous nature of his performances created a unique comedic effect, quickly winning him a devoted following.

His newfound passion became a way to connect with his sister, creating a shared space of creative expression beyond the traditional family gatherings. They began collaborating on various projects, using their differing skill sets to complement each other's work. Leah's artistic visions found life through David's innovative technical solutions, blending their unique talents into dynamic projects that seamlessly incorporated art, technology, and storytelling. Their shared experiences, infused with a healthy dose of self-deprecating humor, became the foundation of their creative synergy.

Their individual achievements, however, were never divorced from the family experiences that had shaped them. They remained deeply connected to their parents, their successes a testament to the values and support they had received throughout their lives. They understood that their accomplishments weren't solely their own; they were a reflection of the unique family dynamic that had nurtured them, a family that had embraced its imperfections and celebrated its diversity. They had learned to appreciate the messy, unpredictable, and often hilarious journey of their blended family, recognizing that their individual journeys were inextricably interwoven with the collective narrative of their family.

Family gatherings continued to be a vibrant tapestry of cultural exchanges and humorous mishaps. Christmas dinners remained a delightful mix of Southern comfort food and Scandinavian delicacies, a testament to the enduring fusion of cultures within their family. Thanksgiving remained a potential culinary disaster, but it was also a time for laughter and shared memories. My mother's attempts at mastering the art of lutefisk still resulted in more questions than answers, but the effort itself had become a source of family amusement.

The children's partners became an integral part of the extended family, their unique backgrounds further enriching the already diverse mix. There were initial adjustments, of course – navigating the nuances of cultural differences and family dynamics – but their willingness to embrace the family's unique quirks and traditions created an environment where everyone felt valued and accepted. The shared laughter, the inside jokes, the collective storytelling, all contributed to forging even stronger bonds within the family.

The children's marriages brought new generations into the mix, further expanding the familial circle. Grandchildren were born, adding yet another layer to the complex yet loving family dynamic. These new additions brought with them their own unique perspectives, adding new threads to the ever-evolving tapestry of our family. The challenges remained, of course. Raising children in a multi-cultural environment presented its own set of complexities, demanding constant compromise, empathy, and a shared commitment to tolerance and understanding. Yet, through it all, the family's resilience remained unshaken, their bonds strengthened by the shared experiences and the shared laughter that had been a constant companion throughout their journey. The family had evolved, adapted, and ultimately thrived, creating a legacy of love and laughter that echoed through generations. The lessons learned during those early years of navigating cultural differences and blended family dynamics had been instrumental in shaping their children into individuals who embraced diversity and celebrated the beauty of imperfection. The unconventional family structure, once a source of apprehension, had become their greatest strength, a testament to the power of love and laughter in overcoming adversity. Their story became a testament to the enduring strength of unconventional families, a reminder that love, acceptance, and a healthy dose of humor could conquer any challenge, weaving a rich and vibrant tapestry of familial connections.

The years that followed saw our family blossom into a vibrant, multi-generational tapestry. Leah and David's lives, while diverging in their professional paths, remained deeply intertwined with the family narrative. Leah, now a successful artist with international recognition, continued to draw inspiration from her unique upbringing. Her work evolved, moving beyond the playful depictions of cultural clashes to explore deeper themes of identity, belonging, and the enduring power of family. Her paintings became increasingly abstract, yet the underlying narrative of her family's journey remained palpable – a vibrant symphony of colours and textures reflecting the complexities and beauty of their shared experience. She even began incorporating family photographs into her mixed media pieces, using them as a backdrop for her abstract explorations. A series of works featuring blurry images of family gatherings superimposed with vibrant splashes of colour became her signature style, a testament to both the chaos and joy of her upbringing.

David, meanwhile, reached new heights in his career. His software solutions were being adopted by global corporations, lauded for their innovative approach to bridging cultural divides and fostering seamless communication in diverse teams. He even began mentoring young software engineers, sharing his unique insights on the intersection of technology and human connection. He found a particular satisfaction in helping young people from diverse backgrounds find their place in the tech world, a reflection of his own experience navigating the complexities of a blended family. His evenings, however, were still dedicated to the community theater, where he continued to hone his comedic skills, often incorporating new family anecdotes into his performances. He found that the family's ever-evolving dynamic provided an endless source of comedic inspiration.

The arrival of grandchildren marked a new chapter in our family saga. The children, raised within a melting pot of cultures, embraced their unique heritage with remarkable ease. They were exposed to a kaleidoscope of traditions, languages, and perspectives, growing up fluent not only in English but also in rudimentary Danish and a charmingly accented Southern drawl. Their understanding of diversity was not theoretical; it was woven into the fabric of their everyday lives. They saw their own heritage mirrored in the faces of their cousins, uncles, and aunts, fostering a profound appreciation for the richness of human experience.

Family gatherings evolved into elaborate multicultural feasts. Christmas Eve celebrations now incorporated traditional Danish Julbord (Christmas buffet) alongside a Southern-style ham and collard greens. Thanksgiving became a culinary adventure, blending Scandinavian smørrebrød (open-faced sandwiches) with traditional turkey and stuffing – a testament to the family's ability to reconcile seemingly disparate culinary traditions. These gatherings weren't just meals; they were immersive cultural experiences, offering a glimpse into the unique tapestry of our family's history. Children would happily switch between speaking Danish, explaining the intricacies of a particular Danish dish, and then launching into a lively discussion about the historical significance of the Southern-style sweet potato pie.

The next generation's partners brought new perspectives, languages, and traditions into the fold. Each new addition was greeted with warmth and acceptance, further enriching the vibrant cultural mix. Initial awkwardness was replaced with laughter and shared experiences. Even the inevitable cultural misunderstandings were met with amusement, highlighting the family's growing ability to find humor in the complexities of their diverse heritage. Family dinners became a stage for multilingual conversations, impromptu storytelling sessions, and lively debates about the merits of various cultural traditions.

One memorable Thanksgiving, a heated discussion erupted about the best way to prepare gravy, pitting the Southern family's preference for a rich, creamy gravy against the Scandinavian family's more subdued approach. What started as a friendly debate quickly evolved into a full-blown culinary competition, with each side determined to prove the superiority of their gravy recipe. The ensuing laughter and friendly rivalry, however, only served to cement the family's bond.

The differences in parenting styles initially caused a stir. My mother's meticulous approach to childcare clashed with my father's more relaxed, Southern-style parenting. The grandparents, each with their own set of expectations, often had different ideas about discipline and childhood development. But through it all, a shared love and respect for each other ensured that these differences became topics of lighthearted family discussions rather than sources of major conflict.

What truly defined our family dynamic was not the absence of conflict but rather our shared ability to navigate it with laughter and understanding. The ability to find humor in our differences – be it culinary styles, parenting philosophies, or differing cultural perspectives – became a cornerstone of our collective identity. It was this shared sense of humor, coupled with a profound respect for one another, that allowed us to thrive as a multi-generational, multicultural family. The children, in turn, developed an impressive ability to navigate their own complex social worlds. They were skilled at bridging cultural divides, demonstrating empathy, understanding, and a playful humor that disarmed prejudice and fostered connections.

The family's annual summer vacation became a testament to their ability to navigate diverse preferences. One year, they opted for a Scandinavian-themed cruise along the Norwegian fjords, complete with traditional Danish pastries and midnight sun viewing. The following year, a trip to the Southern United States allowed for a deep dive into American history and culture, culminating in a lively family barbecue. These vacations, meticulously planned to incorporate everyone's interests, proved that the family's diverse heritage was not a source of division but rather a catalyst for creating lasting memories.

Over time, the family's shared history became a rich source of storytelling, passed down through generations. The stories of cultural clashes, culinary experiments, and unexpected moments of joy became cherished family traditions, creating a common thread that connected everyone. These stories were told and retold at every gathering, reinforcing the family's identity and strengthening their bonds.

As the years passed, and our family expanded even further, the underlying theme remained consistent. Our unconventional family structure, once a source of worry and apprehension, had evolved into our greatest strength. It was a testament to the enduring power of love, acceptance, and a healthy dose of humor. The laughter echoed through generations, a symphony of joyful chaos that affirmed our unique identity and celebrated the vibrant, diverse tapestry of our lives. The legacy we were creating was not just one of blood, but of shared experiences, of laughter, of love, and of an unwavering commitment to embracing our diverse heritage. It was a legacy, we hoped, that would endure for generations to come, proving that a family's strength lies not in its conformity but in its unique and beautifully unconventional spirit.

The annual family reunion, held this year at Leah's sprawling art studio in the heart of Brooklyn, was a spectacle. Guests spilled out onto the cobblestone streets, a vibrant mix of ethnicities and ages, their laughter echoing against the brick buildings. Leah, radiant in a flowing bohemian dress, greeted each arrival with a warm hug, her eyes sparkling with pride. David, ever the comedian, was already holding court in the courtyard, regaling a group of giggling grandchildren with exaggerated tales of his early dating days with Leah – tales liberally embellished with slapstick humor and wildly inaccurate details, much to the delight of his audience.

The studio itself was a testament to Leah's success. Massive canvases depicting swirling abstracts hung alongside framed photographs, capturing candid moments from their unconventional family history. One particularly striking piece featured a hazy image of a chaotic Thanksgiving dinner, a whirlwind of outstretched hands, flying gravy boats, and contented smiles – a visual representation of their family's chaotic but loving dynamic. Guests wandered through the gallery, pointing out familiar faces and sharing memories sparked by Leah's artistic interpretations of their lives.

The food, as always, was a multicultural feast. A long table groaned under the weight of Danish pastries, Southern fried chicken, spicy Jamaican jerk chicken, and an assortment of international dishes contributed by family members from all corners of the globe. The aroma alone was a sensory symphony, a testament to their shared culinary heritage and their ability to blend diverse traditions seamlessly. Even the dessert table was a spectacle, featuring both traditional Danish æbleskiver (apple fritters) and a Southern pecan pie, side by side, peacefully coexisting.

As the afternoon wore on, the atmosphere became more relaxed. Grandchildren, their faces smeared with cake, chased each other around the studio, a miniature echo of the family's vibrant, chaotic energy. Parents, relieved from the pressures of hosting, leaned back, sharing stories and laughter. The grandparents, their faces etched with years of shared experiences, watched with pride, their eyes twinkling with affection.

The evening culminated in a family talent show, a tradition that had emerged organically from the family's inherent theatricality. David, naturally, was the master of ceremonies, his jokes riffing off the day's events and the eccentricities of the family members. Leah's sister, a talented singer, belted out a soulful rendition of a Danish folk song, followed by a grandson who performed a mesmerizing breakdancing routine, his movements a fluid blend of cultures and styles. Even the typically shy members of the family were coaxed onto the makeshift stage, showcasing hidden talents and surprising everyone with their hidden abilities. The event was a celebration not just of individual achievements but of the family's collective spirit, their shared ability to laugh at themselves and to celebrate the beauty of their differences.

Beyond the joyous spectacle of the reunion, however, lay a deeper understanding of their shared accomplishment. It wasn't simply about individual success; it was about building a family that defied expectations, a family forged in the crucible of cultural clashes and societal prejudices. Leah's art career, for example, had become a powerful statement against stereotypes. Her work, often featuring powerful, unapologetically Black figures alongside strong, independent white figures, challenged viewers to reassess their preconceived notions about race and family. Her success was not just personal; it was a collective victory for a family that had boldly shattered racial barriers.

David's career trajectory also mirrored this success. His software, originally designed to bridge cultural divides in the workplace, had become a significant force in promoting intercultural understanding on a global scale. He had not only overcome personal prejudice but had actively sought to dismantle it, creating a platform for communication and collaboration that transcended boundaries. The recognition he received wasn't merely for his technical skills, but for his commitment to bridging divides and building a more inclusive world.

The children, raised in this uniquely diverse environment, had inherited their parents' resilience and open-mindedness. They were comfortable navigating a multitude of cultural contexts, fluent in multiple languages, and capable of forging friendships across ethnic and social divides. Their success wasn't merely academic or professional; it was a testament to their ability to embrace complexity, to value diversity, and to find humor in the inevitable cultural misunderstandings. Their adaptability and empathy were a direct result of the environment their parents had so carefully cultivated.

Even the initial skepticism and prejudice from extended family members had, over time, softened into grudging admiration. While not everyone had fully embraced the family's unconventional dynamic, the overwhelming success and happiness of Leah and David, coupled with the undeniable charm of their children and grandchildren, had gradually eroded much of the resistance. The evidence of a thriving, multi-cultural family, so clearly a source of joy and fulfillment, was hard to ignore. It was a powerful counter-narrative to the societal pressures that had attempted to divide them.

The success of this unconventional family wasn't just a story of overcoming prejudice; it was also a testament to the power of love and acceptance. The family's enduring strength stemmed from their ability to laugh together, to celebrate their differences, and to find joy in the midst of the inevitable challenges. Their love, so deeply rooted in shared experiences and mutual respect, proved to be stronger than any societal barrier or familial resistance. It was a love that nurtured, strengthened, and ultimately triumphed.

The legacy they were creating was a radical departure from the norms, a testament to the beauty of diversity and the transformative power of unconditional love. It was a story of laughter, resilience, and the unwavering belief in the strength of a family united by affection and a shared sense of humor, regardless of the color of their skin or the cultural background from which they came. It was a legacy that would inspire generations to come, proving that unconventional families could not only survive but thrive, and that love, in all its forms, was the ultimate force of nature. Their journey, filled with laughter, challenges, and unwavering love, had proved that the most unconventional families could forge the strongest bonds, celebrating their differences and creating a legacy that would endure for generations to come. The story of their success wasn't just theirs; it was a story for everyone who dared to love beyond the confines of expectation.

The legacy of Marcus and Sarah wasn't etched in stone tablets or enshrined in grand monuments; it was woven into the fabric of their family, a vibrant tapestry of laughter, love, and unwavering acceptance. It wasn't a carefully planned inheritance; it was a spontaneous outpouring of their shared values, passed down through generations not with formal lectures, but through the everyday rituals and shared experiences that defined their lives.

Their children, raised in the heart of the 1990s cultural melting pot, absorbed their parents' values like sponges. They saw firsthand the power of embracing differences, not as obstacles, but as enriching additions to their lives. Witnessing their parents' unwavering commitment to each other, despite societal expectations and family pressures, instilled in them a deep sense of self-acceptance and a profound respect for others. Family dinners weren't just about food; they were a masterclass in tolerance. The lively debates, the clash of cultures represented in their culinary choices – from soul food to Danish pastries – taught them the beauty of diversity and the richness of varied perspectives. Disagreements, inevitable in any family, were handled with a healthy dose of humor and a commitment to finding common ground, skills honed by observing their parents' own approach to conflict resolution.

Their grandchildren, growing up in a world that was (hopefully) becoming increasingly accepting, benefited from this rich heritage. They inherited a legacy not just of tolerance but of active engagement with diversity. They spoke multiple languages, effortlessly navigating different cultural contexts. They were raised to view differences not as something to fear, but as opportunities for understanding and connection. Their childhoods were filled with a cacophony of languages, a potpourri of traditions, and a constant stream of stories from their grandparents' unique lives – stories peppered with laughter, both at the absurd situations they encountered and at their own cultural misunderstandings.

This wasn't simply about a passive acceptance of differences; it was about active participation in creating a more inclusive world. Marcus, a pioneering software engineer, had created a platform that facilitated global communication, breaking down cultural barriers and fostering understanding. His success was a direct result of his own experiences; his software was a tangible manifestation of his commitment to bridging divides. Sarah, a brilliant artist, used her canvases to celebrate diversity, to challenge stereotypes, and to promote a more inclusive vision of family and community. Her art wasn't just aesthetically pleasing; it was a powerful social commentary, a testament to her belief in the beauty of difference.

Their children inherited not only their parents' values, but also their entrepreneurial spirit and their unwavering work ethic. They weren't shielded from the struggles and challenges of life, but they were equipped with the tools to navigate them. They learned the value of hard work, the importance of perseverance, and the strength that comes from supporting each other. They saw their parents not as perfect figures, but as flawed, loving individuals who strived to do their best, to learn from their mistakes, and to create a loving and supportive environment for their family. Their children learned that perfection wasn't the goal; growth and resilience were.

The impact extended beyond their immediate family. Marcus and Sarah's commitment to bridging cultural gaps inspired their friends, their colleagues, and even members of their extended family who initially held reservations. Their actions were a testament to the power of leading by example. Their success, both personally and professionally, was a powerful counter-narrative to the negative stereotypes and prejudices that still persisted in society. They demonstrated that interracial relationships could not only survive, but flourish, creating families that were stronger and more resilient than those bound by rigid societal norms.

Their family reunions were legendary, a joyous celebration of their unique heritage. They were a living embodiment of their values, a microcosm of a world where diversity was not just tolerated, but celebrated. The food, a vibrant mix of culinary traditions, mirrored the richness of their family's diverse backgrounds. The conversations, a lively exchange of ideas and perspectives, showcased their commitment to open communication and mutual respect. The laughter, spontaneous and infectious, was a testament to their shared joy and their ability to find humor even in the midst of challenges.

This legacy wasn't simply about the absence of prejudice; it was about the presence of love, acceptance, and a shared commitment to creating a better world. It was a legacy built on the foundation of laughter, resilience, and unwavering belief in the transformative power of love. It was a legacy of actively working against injustice, not through grand pronouncements or political posturing but through the everyday actions that shaped their lives, their relationships, and the lives of those around them.

It was a legacy that extended far beyond their immediate family, rippling outwards to inspire others to embrace diversity, to challenge prejudice, and to create a world where love conquers all.

Marcus and Sarah's story wasn't just a personal triumph; it was a collective victory for those who dared to defy expectations and to build a family that defied societal norms. Their legacy wasn't simply about creating a happy family; it was about creating a better future, one filled with love, laughter, and the unwavering belief in the power of diversity. It was a legacy of love, a testament to the enduring strength of a family bound not by blood alone, but by a shared commitment to love, tolerance, and the unwavering pursuit of a more just and equitable world. It's a legacy that continues to unfold, shaping the lives of future generations and inspiring others to follow in their footsteps, embracing the beauty of difference and the transformative power of unconditional love. It's a legacy that reminds us that the most unconventional families can create the strongest bonds and the most enduring legacies, proving that love, in all its forms, truly is the ultimate force of nature. Their story is a beacon of hope, a testament to the possibility of a world where love transcends all boundaries, where differences are celebrated, and where families, regardless of their composition, can thrive. It's a legacy that will continue to inspire for generations to come.

The years tumbled by, each one adding another layer to the rich tapestry of the family Marcus and Sarah had created. Their children, now adults with families of their own, carried the torch of their parents' legacy, demonstrating the enduring power of love and acceptance. Family gatherings, once a source of apprehension and nervous laughter, had evolved into joyous celebrations, vibrant testaments to their diverse heritage. The aroma of soul food mingled seamlessly with the scent of Danish pastries, the sounds of English intertwined with Danish and the occasional burst of Swahili, a testament to the rich cultural broth that defined their family.

Grandchildren, the latest generation of this extraordinary family, scampered around, their laughter echoing the carefree spirit of their grandparents. They were fluent in multiple languages, easily navigating the complexities of diverse cultures. They understood that differences were not something to be feared but celebrated, a lesson ingrained in them from their earliest memories. Family stories, brimming with humor and heartfelt moments, were passed down through generations, each anecdote a reminder of the power of embracing one's unique identity and respecting the identities of others.

One particularly memorable family reunion saw a spirited debate erupt over the "correct" way to make a traditional Danish pastry. Sarah, her eyes twinkling with mischief, defended her family's recipe with the fierce passion of a warrior queen, while Marcus, ever the peacemaker, suggested a compromise – a blind taste test, judged by the youngest members of the family. The laughter that ensued was both infectious and endearing, a powerful reminder that even the most passionate disagreements could be resolved with good humor and a shared sense of family.

Beyond the family gatherings, the legacy of Marcus and Sarah extended into the wider community. Their children, inspired by their parents' example, actively worked towards creating a more inclusive and just society. They championed initiatives promoting diversity in education and the workplace, fighting to dismantle systemic barriers and challenge ingrained prejudices. Their collective efforts served as a powerful testament to the ripple effect of a single family's commitment to love and acceptance.

Marcus's software, initially designed to connect people across the globe, had become an indispensable tool for social change. It empowered marginalized communities, fostering dialogue and understanding among groups that might otherwise have remained isolated. His legacy was not confined to the digital realm; it was evident in the lives of countless individuals whose voices were amplified through the platform he had created.

Sarah's art continued to provoke conversation and inspire change. Her canvases, vibrant and thought-provoking, challenged societal norms and promoted a more inclusive vision of beauty and family. Museums around the country featured her work, and her paintings had become highly sought-after collectibles, yet she never lost sight of her initial purpose—using her art as a powerful tool for social change.

Even their extended families, those who initially harbored reservations about their interracial marriage, had come to embrace their unique family unit. Witnessing the strength of their bond and the joy radiating from their family life, they had let go of their prejudices and embraced the diverse tapestry of cultures and traditions that had woven itself into the family's very fabric. Their conversion wasn't a sudden epiphany, but a gradual shift, born out of witnessing the genuine love and acceptance that defined Marcus and Sarah's relationship and the family they'd created.

Their story, initially met with skepticism and resistance from some, had transformed into a beacon of hope. It offered a powerful counter-narrative to the narratives of division and prejudice, demonstrating that interracial families were not merely surviving but thriving. Their legacy was a living testament to the potential for love to overcome obstacles and build bridges across divides.

The final chapter of their story wasn't about a grand finale, a dramatic conclusion, or a perfectly tied-up bow. It was about the quiet, unassuming strength of a family that continued to grow, to evolve, and to inspire. It was about the simple act of loving unconditionally, embracing differences, and actively working to create a world where everyone felt accepted and valued.

Marcus, in his twilight years, sat on his porch, watching the sunset paint the sky in a myriad of colors – a visual metaphor for the beautiful diversity of his family. He smiled, a knowing smile that spoke volumes about the journey they had traveled and the impact they had made. He thought of Sarah, her laughter echoing in his memory, her spirit forever ingrained in the hearts of their children and grandchildren.

Their legacy was not about riches or fame; it was about something far more valuable – a legacy of love, acceptance, and unwavering belief in the transformative power of family. It was a legacy that transcended race, culture, and societal expectations, proving that the strongest bonds are not forged in conformity but in the celebration of differences.

It was a legacy that would continue to unfold, chapter by chapter, year by year, inspiring future generations to embrace diversity, challenge prejudices, and build a world where love conquers all. It was a legacy that proved, beyond a shadow of a doubt, that the most unconventional families can often create the strongest bonds and leave the most enduring impact on the world. Their story, a testament to the enduring power of love, would echo through time, a reminder that even in the face of adversity, love, resilience, and laughter can create a legacy that truly matters. It's a legacy that whispered of hope and a future where difference is not just tolerated, but cherished, a legacy they'd worked tirelessly to create, a legacy woven into the very fabric of their family, a legacy that would ultimately outlive them all. And that, in itself, was a legacy worth celebrating.

Back Matter

First and foremost, a massive shout-out to my incredibly supportive family – you guys are the reason I haven't ended up living in a cardboard box fueled by lukewarm instant coffee and existential dread. Seriously, thanks for putting up with me, even when I was convinced my comedic genius was best expressed through interpretive interpretive dance involving a rubber chicken.

To my agent, bless your cotton socks, for believing in this project when I was still pitching it as a three-hour opera featuring interpretive dance with aforementioned rubber chicken. Your faith in my... unique vision is inspiring.

A huge thank you to my editor, whose patience with my endless stream of puns and questionable life choices is nothing short of saintly. You've shaped this chaotic mess into something... well, less chaotic.

And finally, to the readers: thanks for giving this book a shot. I hope you enjoy it, even if you have to Google half the references. Now go forth and spread the joy (and maybe buy my next book).

Soul Food: Delicious, soul-satisfying food that somehow manages to be both comforting and utterly addictive. (See also: comfort food, deliciousness overload).

Danish Pastries: Exquisitely flaky, buttery pastries of Danish origin. (Often used as a weapon in family disputes, see Chapter 7).

Swahili: A Bantu language spoken in East Africa. (In this book, primarily used for dramatic effect and comedic mispronunciations).

Interracial Marriage: A marriage between people of different racial or ethnic backgrounds. (Still shocking to some, apparently. Get over it).

Made in the USA
Coppell, TX
19 February 2026

72015139R00080